FLY FISHI

Pacific Northwest Waters

John Shewey

TROUT AND BEYOND II

FLY FISHING
Pacific Northwest Waters

John Shewey

TROUT AND BEYOND II

Frank Amato
PORTLAND

Dedication

To DeAnn

Acknowledgments

I wish to thank the people of the Oregon Department of Fish & Wildlife, Washington Department of Wildlife, Idaho Fish & Game Department and Wyoming Wildlife Department for their cooperation in providing me with information for this book. Thanks also to Tim Blount for his continued willingness to involve himself in my merciless avalanche of fly fishing trips, some great, others sheer psychological and physical punishment. A similar thanks must go to Forrest Maxwell, who always seems to be along on those trips where everything works out for the best. And thanks to Dee for putting up with all of it.

©1997 by John Shewey

Published in 1997 by
Frank Amato Publications, Inc.
PO Box 82112
Portland, Oregon 97282
(503) 653-8108

Softbound
ISBN: 1-57188-086-0
UPC: 0-66066-00284-6

All photographs taken by the author unless otherwise noted.
Cover flies tied by John Shewey
Front cover photograph: Jim Schollmeyer
Back cover photograph: John Shewey

Book design: Tony Amato

Printed in Hong Kong

1 3 5 7 9 10 8 6 4 2

CONTENTS

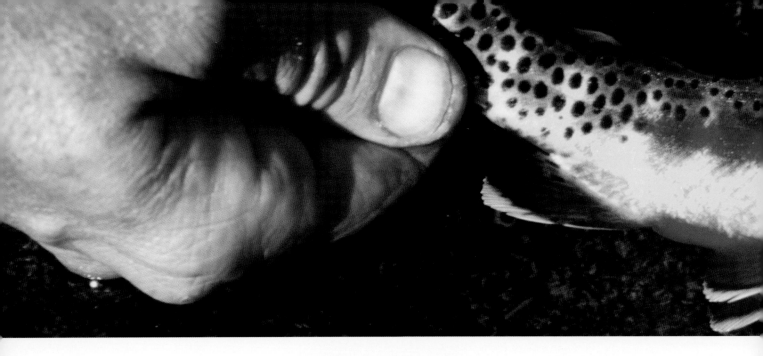

FOREWORD

John Shewey is my hero, and I'll tell you why. Through all his years of fishing—more years than he's entitled to at his young age—John has kept his sense of adventure, his sure sense for exploration, and his sense of wonder at whatever he might catch. You'll capture a hint about this in a sentence from his book: "The same year that I perfected my techniques for freshwater clams, I began hearing rumors about fly-caught catfish in the Snake River near Nampa." You and John are blown away with the wind of that rumor, off on the scent of another adventure.

What we truly fish for is surprise: that sudden connection to something alive beneath the water, and that wonder about what it might be and how big it might be, if and when we get it to the surface. Most times you and John both hope it's something more than a mere clam attached to your fly. But the surprise itself is the quarry, and if the surprise is a clam, only an enlarged sense of wonder will let you appreciate that. The more we develop certainty about what our quarry, and therefore our catch, will be, the more we reduce the chance of capturing surprise, and in a sense the more we deduct from our own catch.

Most of us narrow our list of species, rather than expand it, as we become more experienced anglers. Some specialize in trout, others in steelhead, many in warmwater species such as bluegill and bass. Whichever we choose, we tend to look down our uptilted noses at all the others. If you don't believe me, try telling the story about your last big bluegill to a summer steelheader and watch while his eyes grow dim and distant.

John will tell you lots of stories in this book, about everything from winter steelhead to spring creek trout to schooling crappie, and your eyes are not going to glaze over. He'll do the opposite: open your eyes wide. He opened mine to a mistake I've been making.

In recent years I've been tramping out to the same old places, and improving my ability to catch the same old fish. They're great places, and great fish. All the same, I've been narrowing my list of species, and cramping my sense of adventure. I've been reducing my own chance to capture the very thing that it's most important to catch: surprise.

That's why John is my hero. He has managed to keep his sense of adventure enlarged, and to enlarge mine with his fine writing. In the twelve chapters of his earlier great book, *Northwest Fly Fishing: Trout and Beyond,* John led exploratory trips in precisely a dozen different directions, from deep in the waves of the surf to high in the alpine meadows of the mountains.

In *Flyfishing Pacific Northwest Waters: Trout and Beyond II* John bolts off in ten new directions. I won't hold you up any longer. It's time for you to dash off with him.

Dave Hughes
Portland, Oregon

INTRODUCTION

Well, here we go again—Volume II of *Trout & Beyond*. For those fly anglers among you who enjoyed the original *Trout & Beyond*, I hope this one proves helpful as well. One thing is certain: The Pacific Northwest, from eastern Idaho to the West coast, offers so many different fly angling opportunities, that almost immediately after the release of *Trout & Beyond* back in 1992, I realized a second volume would be needed to really cover the territory, so to speak.

This book might not break as much new ground as the original *Trout & Beyond* did with its chapters on surfperch, bottomfish and shad, but I hope *Trout & Beyond II* proves valuable for its attention to some of the more common yet underutilized species found throughout the Northwest. These include the sunfishes, crappie and largemouth bass. In addition, this book attempts to introduce anglers to some of the opportunities every Western fly fisher deserves to experience—hence the chapters on spring creeks, golden trout and grayling and my favorite hatches.

During one of many the field-research trips for this book, I ran into a problem that I, along with many other Northwest anglers, face just by virtue of where we live. I was bent on photographing some beaver ponds during a trip to Idaho. Unfortunately for my beaver-pond photography, I never quite got there. First Brownlee Reservoir got in the way—how could I pass by Huntington, Oregon without venturing up to the reservoir for a try at some smallmouth bass? I blew a whole day there and then continued on, well after dark, toward my destination. Very early the next morning, after several hours of driving, I pulled into a wide spot along the Big Wood River to sleep for a spell.

I couldn't possibly pass on the Big Wood, so I fished away a morning, after which I figured I might as well go fish Silver Creek since I wouldn't make the beaver-pond country before dark anyway. Silver Creek fished pretty well until about three in the afternoon, at which time I decided to spend the rest of that day fishing one of the high lakes in the mountains northwest of Sun Valley. There I found big, not to mention rather dumb, cutthroat as a reward for a hurried three-mile hike.

Early the next morning I was about to pack up, drive back down to Sun Valley and continue on my way to my favorite beaver ponds over in eastern Idaho. Then logic got the better of me: I was already in Sawtooth Valley. Why not look for beaver ponds here? I spent two days hiking around in the Sawtooths, looking a lot more diligently for lakes full of big cutthroat than for beaver ponds. The end result of that trip included not a single beaver-pond photo and I didn't really care. After all, that's the kind of problem I like to have: So much opportunity for good fishing that I can't decide what to do next.

Forrest Maxwell and I were discussing the possibilities for autumn fishing one year. I suggested Nevada. He liked that idea. He suggested our favorite lake in the Mt. Jefferson Wilderness. I liked that idea. I then offered Deschutes River steelhead and he countered with our beloved little desert trout streams. Of course the North Santiam was still fishing pretty well. Then we remembered that bird season would coincide with all these plans. Forrest threw his hands in the air, saying, "I know damn well I'm going to die of stress one of these years—too many decisions to be made!"

He was right, of course. Perhaps not about dying of stress, but about having so many choices. So if you are bound and determined to die of stress from having too many choices for fly fishing destinations, then I'd be honored if this book helps send you on your way!

John Shewey
Bend, Oregon

Chapter I

Beaver Ponds

A beaver works on his lodge in a stream in Idaho's Caribou Mountains.

For years I've maintained a love-hate relationship with range bulls—basically they tend to hate me and seem to love the idea of maiming me.

As a youngster, in fact, I excelled at track, primarily the sprints—a fact which I'm certain was the only positive development from my relationship with behemoth range bulls.

There was one bull in particular: A crusty old Hereford that outweighed most Chevy products and snorted venomous breath that could peel the paint off a jeep at 50 yards. I can attest to the quality of the beast's oral hygiene on account of being held at bay in a rather flimsy aspen tree for the better part of an afternoon.

A Hereford is generally not the most ill-tempered of range bulls (unfortunately I've had the opportunity to compare relative aggressiveness among breeds), but Old Red, as we used to call him, had a dislike for the world in general, and for me in particular. I have no doubt he could have reduced the meanest drill sergeant to a heap of shivering putty with a mere pawing of the ground and a menacing snort or two. Any conquistador would have retired from the game rather than face a monster like Old Red. When he wasn't busy bowling over fenceposts, aspens, and other like objects, or pushing the other bulls around, he was probably sitting on a rock somewhere filing his horns to needle-sharp points while puffing on a cheap cigar stub.

You might think it best if I had just avoided his territory altogether. But that strategy has two obvious flaws. For starters, I was never that smart; more importantly, the sprawl-ing high desert range occupied by Old Red just happened to be drained by three streams, each one featuring beaver ponds stacked together like stairs in a staircase—one pond after another after another. All were filled with native cutthroat, always willing and sometimes large.

Eat, sleep, fish; eat, sleep, fish. That was the drill all summer long in those days with those creeks all located within walking distance for a kid severely impaired by fly fishing fever. Old Red was just one more hurdle in my development as a fly angler and I learned early on to give him a wide berth (minimum of at least two major mountain ranges between us would have been ideal, but I frequently had to settle for a few hundred yards and several Hail Mary's).

I always kept an eye peeled, no matter how good the fishing. And the fishing could be nothing short of furious at times. Mostly I fished alone, although one summer day I took a neighbor kid along with me. We hiked to the upper reaches of the furthest creek and hammered cutthroat continuously all afternoon. We camped near the headwaters of that creek so we could climb over the divide first thing the next morning and fish our way down the next creek.

By sun-up we were casting hopper patterns into beaver ponds teeming with trout that had awaited our arrival with mouths watering. My favorite of all the beaver ponds lay along that creek.

This pond was magical. Where most of the others were always slightly off color, this one was gin clear, owing to the springs that fed directly into the bottom of the pond. A lush carpet of bright green weeds and deep green mosses lined the pond's bottom, yielding to clean, grayish gravel where the springs pumped cool water into the pool. Big cutthroat, clearly visible, cruised the pond, sampling the bountiful food supply at leisure.

It was a large beaver pond, S-shaped, and hugging a steep, willow-clad slope on one side. That incline, combined with a four-foot-high cut bank running the pond's length on the near side, kept cattle out. The Herefords did, however, like to drink from the next pond downstream.

That was this incredible pond's only downfall. You could bump into that damn bull anytime in the concealing brush on the wide bench adjacent to the creek.

Naturally, that fact weighed heavily on our young minds as we nervously stalked across the bench toward the pond, which lay a good quarter mile off the trail.

A half-dozen young Hereford steers, surprised by our sudden appearance, scattered noisily through the chokecherries and willows as we neared the pond. We froze, expecting Old Red to emerge through the brush at any moment. Nothing more stirred. My friend helped pry my fingers from the aspen I was about to climb and we continued toward the creek.

We reached the pond, its surface glistening in tranquility. We groped our way out onto the large beaver dam, mindful of our footing to avoid taking a beaver-chewed stick through the leg. From atop the dam we could easily fish the entire lower end of the pond. Almost immediately we were both into decent trout. Shortly after we clubbed these fish (catch and release wasn't exactly a buzz word at that time) a pair of Herefords sloshed through the stream below the dam, just a few yards away. We froze, hoping they were alone. A few minutes passed and we eventually remembered to breathe again.

All was quiet after that and we proceeded to put the hurt on the trout in the lower end of the pond. Then we fished our way up the near side, carefully ducking through the willows at selected spots and making short flip casts into the clear water. A few short twitches of the fly and the trout would run each other down to get there first.

The upper end of the pond, where the stream's influence created a slight current, always held a 16- or 18-inch trout. Since my friend had not seen this place before, I generously offered to go ahead and fish it myself so he could observe my technique for future reference.

The still of mid-morning intimated another perfect August day. Birds sang cheerfully from the nearby trees, undisturbed by our presence, and we had all but forgotten about Old Red.

I eased carefully through the willows, keeping very low and trying to blend with the shadows. This upper section of the pond, shrouded in riparian shrubbery, meandered in a narrow S-curve before stretching to its full width below. I weaseled into a reasonable casting position and uncorked my fly. At precisely that moment, a tremendous "ker-splush" erupted from the pond very close by.

Later, when my friend caught up with me a ways down the trail and located the aspen in which I was perched (thereafter he said he understood the name "quaking aspen"), he said he'd never seen a beaver slap its tail on the water before and was surprised at how loud it sounded.

I assured him I knew it was a beaver all along and was just trying to liven up the morning with some good-natured

humor. We collected my various items of tackle and equipment, which I had discarded rather suddenly, and fished the next couple of beaver ponds.

The rest of the morning passed without incident and we caught dozens of fat cutthroat from those beaver ponds. We fished all the way down that creek, in fact, to within two canyons and a winter wheat field of my house. It was late afternoon by then, so we elected to make the trek home, having each killed a half-dozen trout to show off to our respective families.

After cleaning our trout, we finally left the creek, ascended a slight hill and relocated the trail, dead in the middle of which stood Old Red.

To this day I'm not sure who reached home first, but I do know that I finally had some serious competition in the sprints that fall in seventh grade track. And I also know that despite the menacing presence of that old Hereford bull, we continued to fish those creeks, drawn by the promise of eager cutthroat in those magical beaver ponds.

Finding Beaver Ponds

The best beaver-pond fishing I have encountered has been in the Rocky Mountain states, where remote cottonwood- and aspen-lined streams make ideal beaver habitat. To find these places, I consult a national forest map, looking for year-round streams that drain small mountain valleys, basins and canyons.

Then I consult the USGS topo maps, which are larger scale and thus show more detail, and check for gentle slopes and, in some cases, the presence of marsh areas along the creeks. When topo maps indicate marshlands along the mountain creeks, these generally turn out to be beaver ponds. One caution: Many USGS maps are dated and might not reflect the current reality. Beavers only occupy a stream as long as their food supply is adequate and at times, over a number of years, can eat themselves out of a home.

In any event, areas of relatively gentle gradient are better suited to productive beaver ponds than are steep-sloping streams. If, on a Forest Service map, a main stream is fed by numerous small, very short tributaries, you can usually bet that this particular creek occupies very steep country. On the other hand, if a map shows a stream meandering somewhat and fed by meandering tributaries, the area probably deserves investigation. I've fished a lot of beaver pond country in eastern and central Idaho where beavers are common and where small streams with gentle slopes frequently offer long series' of ponds, one after another, sometimes spanning a mile or more. In any case, a U.S. Geological Survey topographical map (7.5-minute series if available) will help a great deal in deciphering the kind of terrain you are investigating.

If you explore one canyon or mountain valley without finding beaver ponds, try the next canyon over or try the other side of the range. Also remember that on most Rocky Mountain streams, beaver ponds are more likely to be found near the stream headwaters than downstream near agriculture or ranching operations. In fact, if you can locate a divide, where two or three streams flow toward different sides of the range, you will frequently find each to offer several beaver ponds near their respective headwaters, especially if the divide is somewhat flat at the top. In any event, with a little map work, you shouldn't have much trouble locating beaver country in the Rockies, especially if you stick to more remote areas with lots of aspen and cottonwood growth.

The mountains of Washington and Oregon offer beaver ponds as well, but you must look a little harder to find them, especially in the Cascades. Still, a good topo map can help you locate likely drainages and you can consult district Forest Service personnel who know the area. Remember also that some of the less obtrusive mountain ranges in the Northwest contain ample populations of beaver.

Strategies and Tactics for Beaver Ponds

Beaver ponds offer a unique opportunity to practice both moving-water and still-water tactics on the same body of water. In effect, they are miniature reservoirs, yet most maintain a small-stream flavor simply because they exist as part of the small-creek ecosystem. One minute you can cast hopper imitations as if fishing a stream; the next, you can retrieve a damsel nymph as you would in a lake. In either case you can expect good results.

Trout foods associated with still waters are quick to take hold in beaver ponds. These include the damselflies as well as dragonflies, *Callibaetis* mayflies, scuds, leeches and water beetles. At the same time, beaver ponds frequently support populations of creatures generally encountered on moving water, including *Baetis* (and *Pseudocloeon*) mayflies (commonly called blue-winged olives or tiny western olives), terrestrials, like ants, beetles and hoppers, various caddis, even small stoneflies.

Thus we end up with waters in which a fly angler might need to fish any in a wide array of techniques. Luckily, however, all this is tempered by the fact that most beaver ponds are inhabited by trout that are conditioned to feed opportunistically most of the time. In other words, beaver-pond trout are not picky very often.

This is partly due to the fact that, despite the variety of food organisms available, many beaver ponds don't support overly large populations of any given food item. Still, some ponds can grow and sustain big trout. Often, of course, you will find beaver ponds loaded with small trout, especially when brook trout are involved, but many other ponds contain a pleasant mixture of small and medium-sized trout with an occasional lunker thrown in to keep things interesting. Sizes are relative, of course. A 16- or 18-inch fish is a hell of a trout in most high-country beaver ponds.

Often the best place from which to cast to beaver-pond trout is from just below the dam itself. Here the author casts to visible trout cruising in this Oregon beaver pond.

Hidden by her position below the dam and well back in the shadows, this angler can cast to beaver-pond trout without spooking them.

A few years ago, during a hunting trip in Idaho, I took an afternoon to fish a string of beaver ponds that I found while looking for good ruffed grouse cover. The first pond yielded a half-dozen cutthroat and two rainbows, the largest being a fat 12-incher. As I progressed further upstream, however, the trout kept averaging a little larger. The travel got worse and worse as well. The stream meandered through a narrow basin that was little more than a tangle of willows and chokecherries—so much so that just getting from one pond to the next was a real challenge.

Near the top of the basin a few aspens lined both sides of the stream. I eventually reached this place and found a long, narrow beaver pond from which I caught an 18-inch and a 20-inch cutthroat. I would have never expected fish like that from a smallish, high-altitude beaver pond, but you never know. I might add, by the way, that, with my shotgun awaiting me back at the truck, I flushed three ruffed grouse near the top of that upper pond.

The ponds I fished that day were slightly off-color, a situation that you will encounter on occasion. Most ponds are pristine and clear. I've never found the relative clarity to have much to do with the size or quantity of trout available, so don't let that slight green-gray color of cattle-country beaver ponds fool you.

Clear water or not, beaver ponds require a careful approach. Some ponds feature cut banks and steep drop-offs—even undercut banks—with trout cruising very near shore. Others require that you wade through shallow, grass-choked marshes before you can cast into the deeper, open water. In either case, you must approach slowly and with a low profile to avoid spooking trout.

As a 10-year-old kid I discovered a beaver pond that required extraordinary measures. Cattle had grazed most of the grass away from the tall bank on the only approachable side, so walking or even crawling to the water's edge was out. Instead, I soon learned that I had to lay flat on my belly and squirm toward the pond like a snake to get within reach of the school of hungry cutthroat waiting below. When feeding, this school of 30 or so trout would simply line up near the top of the pond, where a slight current pushed food down from above. A few adventurous individuals always cruised freely about the pond and these were the fish that would alert the others to my presence if I so much as lifted my head too high.

Sometimes the easiest way to negotiate soggy beaver-pond meadows is to walk across the dams themselves.
Not to worry—any damage done to the dam will be repaired overnight by the perpetually busy beavers.

It was totally blind fishing. When I reached a position some six feet away from the bank, I would roll over on my back and flip a short cast backward into the pond. The instant my fly hit the water it would be attacked. Only then would I know if my stalk had been successful. If nothing happened, I would carefully raise my head, only to see all the trout balled together at the bottom of the pond, obviously frightened by some minor error in my approach.

I discovered very early on that the best approach to most beaver ponds was from below the dam itself, but this was impossible on this particular pond so I had to settle for second best. Those trout would only remain frightened for five minutes or so and would then return to their feeding stations. If I hooked a trout on the first cast, I had only to land it, wait five minutes for the remaining fish to recover from their fright, and then make the approach all over again.

This was an extreme case, but it does illustrate the potential for spooky trout in many beaver ponds, especially during the low-water period of late summer.

In a few places, I have found beaver-pond trout that are virtually unspookable: In every case these fish have resided in ponds that are frequented by range cattle—I think the fish get so used to all the commotion caused by the cattle that they simply refuse to be put down at the sight of a large body moving about on the banks. I first discovered this situation quite by accident in some beaver ponds in Oregon's Fremont National Forest. Cattle ran amok along the meadow section of this particular creek. I wanted to see how big the trout grew, so I just ambled up to the side of a deep pond channel and peered into the water, looking for trout. At my initial approach a school of some two dozen brook trout scurried about in apparent panic. Immediately, however, the fish re-schooled

and settled back into their holding area with me in plain view the whole time.

Naturally I wondered whether these trout would now chase a fly with me standing above them. I uncorked a little Zug Bug, flip-cast it into the pond above the school of trout, and watched several fish rise eagerly toward the fly. The tiny dimple caused by the fly landing on the water had apparently triggered their interest. The largest fish in the school—a monstrous nine-incher—inhaled the Zug Bug before I had even bothered to impart any action on the slowly sinking fly.

An abundance of cattle comprised the common element in each case where I encountered such emboldened beaver-pond trout. Talk about easy marks—not only were the fish unselective, but you couldn't spook them no matter how hard you tried. Don't count on this to be the case very often, however, as most beaver-pond trout act as spooky as any fish you are likely to encounter.

As mentioned above, the best approach to most ponds is from below the dam itself. By sneaking in below the dam, you can often cover the entire lower end of a large pond with nothing more than your head and shoulders—if that—potentially visible to the trout. Virtually every serious beaver-pond angler with whom I have discussed the subject has agreed that this is the best approach for most ponds. In addition, any beaver-pond regular would instruct you to fish the tailrace of these dams before wading in to fish the pond above.

Some small ponds can be covered thoroughly from below the dam. If not, then I work my way along one side, usually the edge offering better casting positions. Satisfied I have fished a pond thoroughly, I then wade into the tailrace of the next dam (remembering to fish this tailwater first) and go through the same process.

Obviously, this tactic requires that I begin at the lower reaches of a string of beaver ponds and work my way upstream. Given a reasonable number of ponds, one can easily tie up an entire day this way.

In addition, I frequently use the dams themselves as bridges for crossing from one side to another. Footing can be tricky because once in a while a small part of a dam will sag under your weight, although very rarely will you collapse more than a tiny fragment of the dam. Usually you will find these sturdy structures to make excellent bridges. One caution: Be very careful on new dams or those recently renovated because they are not entirely solid until completely finished by the beavers. Fresh-cut bows and limbs, sometimes with green leaves still attached, in addition to fresh mud and piles of fresh leaves lining parts of the dam, indicate works in progress.

Incidentally, you needn't worry about minor damage that you may cause to a dam by walking on it because the beavers will almost invariably repair the structure overnight. (The late George Heinold, whose nature profile stories used to appear in *Sports Afield*, once reported that a beaver could down a five-inch aspen in three minutes.)

Naturally, when considering your approach to a particular beaver pond, you should bear in mind that trout prefer certain places in any given pond. The tails of the ponds usually hold trout, especially where overhanging willows crowd the edges of the dam. Many ponds feature a channel that marks the original streambed. Trout hold and cruise in such channels because of the security offered by the deeper water.

In addition, many beaver ponds are bordered by dense riparian vegetation and, in many cases, cut banks. The shadows provided in such places often harbor trout, sometimes covered by only a few inches of water.

Finally, as mentioned earlier, trout frequently reside in the tailraces of beaver dams, so never overlook these areas. At times you'll take the best trout of the day from the cool water of the tailrace.

Usually the best beaver ponds, or at least those holding the largest trout, feature areas of fairly deep water (four feet or considerably more) and offer ample cover to the trout. In addition, if larger trout are your quest, look for drainages dominated by cutthroat or the occasional drainage harboring brown trout or rainbows. Some Western beaver pond streams are overpopulated with stunted brook trout. Personally, I enjoy the colorful little brookies. They are always aggressive and cooperative, even if rather puny. Besides, once in a while you'll tangle with 16- or 18-inch brook trout while exploring the beaver ponds.

Once you have decided how best to approach a beaver pond or series of ponds you are left with deciding what fishing tactics to employ. My rule is pretty simple: Unless I either (a) see evidence of surface activity to indicate a hatch or (b) am familiar enough with the area to know what will produce, I start with searching patterns. Generally these will be wet flies, except during the grasshopper season when a hopper pattern can work wonders.

My favorite beaver-pond searchers, all meant to be cast and retrieved in the manner of lake fishing, include smallish Woolly Buggers, Carey Specials, Zug Bugs, damsel nymphs, small Muddlers and various soft hackles. I usually fish two at a time—a size 12 peacock Carey Special as the lead and a size 14 Partridge & Orange soft-hackle as the dropper, for example.

In many ponds, dry flies prove just as effective as wet patterns. My favorites include the Parachute Adams, Gulper Special, Renegade, and Griffith's Gnat. Allow the dry fly to sit still on the water for a few seconds. If a trout doesn't rise within 10 or 15 seconds, gently skate the fly on the surface by

The author leisurely fishes an old beaver pond under the tranquility of a summer evening in the Rockies.

stripping in line. Often enough, trout will turn a back flip to get at a dry fly, but if you can't prompt the fish to rise, then switch to the wet flies.

You never want to ignore the obvious, of course. I've walked up on ponds where water beetles and backswimmers were everywhere, in which case I used the appropriate imitation. Similarly, I've often chosen damsel nymphs simply because of the voluminous aquatic vegetation in a particular pond. But barring the obvious, attractor patterns are the way to go, at least for starters. Incidentally, some ponds are so full of hungry trout that you can't help but hook two fish on the same retrieve (one on each fly). Using three flies I've hooked a triple, but I have yet to try for four.

Sometimes feeding patterns are evident and you need only match the hatch. I've fished over prolific mayfly emergences on some ponds. The *Callibaetis* mayfly is common on some waters, as are small blue-winged olives (*Baetis* and *Pseudocloeon*), not to mention the giant *Hexagenia* mayfly, which occurs on some beaver ponds.

Because beaver-pond trout are rarely ultra-selective, carry a variety of parachute-style dry flies in a range of sizes and two or three colors. These will suffice for most mayfly hatches you are likely to encounter. My favorite is the Troth Gulper Special.

Similarly, a variety of Elk Hair Caddis flies cover the caddis emergences on beaver ponds. These are especially effective when greased well with floatant and skated slowly or twitched across the surface. During heavy caddis emergences a soft-hackle wet fly often outfishes the Elk Hair or other dry pattern.

Despite the hatches associated with beaver ponds, terrestrial patterns often prove to be the most significant dry flies. Toss a live grasshopper into the middle of a beaver pond and you'll see what I mean. Because most beaver ponds are located above 5,000 feet in the Rockies and other ranges, the fishing doesn't really start until mid to late June, sometimes later still. Thus the peak season for beaver ponds—July through September—coincides with the peak abundance of hoppers, beetles and ants.

Hoppers are especially fun to fish because beaver-pond trout often explode on them violently, especially in ponds that are loaded with trout. Even in less densely populated ponds, trout are eager to take hopper imitations. I fished a clear-water pond a few years ago that appeared devoid of fish. Not over three feet deep anywhere, the pond offered only one old root wad as cover for trout. I pitched a hopper onto the surface about five feet from the root wad and watched a 20-inch cutthroat casually glide from beneath the sunken mass of roots, inhale the fly in a slow, deliberate gulp and turn back toward its hiding place. That was one of the most exciting trout I have ever caught in a beaver pond.

Perhaps the most productive hopper technique is to cast the fly below overhanging vegetation, allowing the fly to land with a soft "splat." Wait until the ripples clear, then if a trout hasn't already demolished the fly, give the line a series of short pulls to twitch the imitation. Any beaver-pond trout bent on eating hoppers won't be able to resist.

Ants and beetles are favorites of beaver-pond trout as well, especially along forested ponds. I once cleaned a pair of dinner trout from an Idaho beaver pond and found both fish to be stuffed with small beetles and black ants. During late summer this is not unusual.

Toward the end of the season, streamers can be deadly in beaver ponds, especially those harboring brook trout and/or

In lush mountain meadows where trout rarely see humans or cattle, the fish require the utmost caution and stealth on the angler's part.

brown trout. Marabou Muddlers are my favorites, although just about any streamer, from a Mickey Finn to a Woolhead Sculpin, will do the trick on spawning-season brookies and marauding, hungry browns.

One other dry fly tactic that can prove deadly on beaver ponds is to cast adult damsel imitations onto the water, let them sit until the ripples clear, and then impart an occasional twitch. Frequently you won't have to wait long enough to impart the first twitch. The damselfly hatch usually peaks early to mid-July but continues in lower densities into August. Throughout the actual hatch period, damsel nymphs are deadly, especially during the morning migration period from around 9 a.m. until the emergence is in full swing an hour or two later. As the hatch begins, adult imitations become productive. Also, when adult damsels swarm over the water during mating flights, beaver-pond trout are eager to eat any that happen to end up in the water. I've even watched trout try to snare adult damsels in the air.

Luckily, beaver-pond trout rarely act selective toward foods they take from the surface. Therefore, some general dry fly patterns will fool these fish almost any time they seem surface-oriented. As they do in lakes, trout frequently cruise around beaver ponds searching for prey and are all too happy to take a swipe at anything that looks edible.

If you approach a beaver pond and see a trout or two rising every few minutes, you can usually take these fish on a dry fly if you so choose. A size 14 Griffith's Gnat or Renegade works wonders on these non-selective risers. Using a long leader, make a delicate cast toward the area where the fish are rising most consistently. Allow the ripples caused by your cast to clear from the water. Then gently pull on the line to make the fly inch forward, causing a very subtle wake. After each gentle twitch, allow the fly to sit motionless for a few seconds then repeat the process. To the trout, a fly fished in this manner must look like a struggling insect trapped in the surface film. Even though a wet fly could take these non-selective risers as well or better, I find it hard to pass up the chance to rise them to a dry.

In any event, a quiet, careful approach is the key to fishing beaver ponds because the trout are usually spooky and the water is frequently clear as glass. The other constant about beaver ponds is that they will make you work more often than

Even after being abandoned by its creators, this beaver pond held back enough water to provide excellent cover for trout. Beavers will occupy a section of stream only so long as the food supply holds out.

not because they are usually surrounded by a jungle of willows, chokecherries, other shrubs and chewed-off branches left protruding from the ground like so many small spears. But the work is usually worthwhile. In fact some of the best beaver ponds, like anything else, are those that require the most blood, sweat and tears.

Beaver Pond Safety

Beaver ponds can present some serious hazards to the unwary. My friend Tim Blount gouged out a three-inch chunk of his leg on a beaver-chewed willow stub a few years ago. These chewed stubs, often hidden by grass or mud, are the biggest Nemesis of the beaver ponds. They act a lot like an Asian tiger trap: An unsuspecting angler steps into a pond only to have eight inches of sharpened willow limb puncture those expensive waders and perhaps the leg inside.

Other beaver-pond hazards are the holes, burrows and channels dug by the beasts themselves. Properly placed and concealed, these pits can ruin a perfectly good fishing trip (twisted knees and ankles have a way of doing that).

The only defense against beaver-pond hazards, short of beaver traps and dynamite, is extreme caution. Watch your step. Naturally, the minute you start concentrating extra hard on careful wading and stalking, a beaver will sneak up behind you and slap his tail on the water so hard that you'll hope you brought an extra pair of shorts. (If you've had that happen, you know what I'm talking about. If not, just take my word for it: Get the bladder-control scared out of you a time or two by a beaver slapping its tail on the water, you might start thinking seriously about the beaver traps and dynamite.)

The only other real hazard of beaver-pond fishing—and I'm serious about this—is that offered by the inevitable presence of moose along beaver ponds throughout northern, central and eastern Idaho, as well as adjacent Montana and Wyoming. Moose are relatively shy, although somewhat curious at times, but you don't want to sneak around a corner along a beaver-pond stream and position yourself between a mother moose and her calf. I've unwittingly stalked within mere yards of moose along some beaver ponds only to have the moose and myself discover one another at the same instant, each of us reacting with some surprise.

Incidentally, the beavers themselves are almost never aggressive toward humans, although Jimmy Gabettas of Pocatello, Idaho is one of the few to witness the exception to this generality. Jimmy got chased away from a pond by a healthy-sized beaver a few years back, not once but twice.

Beaver Pond Tackle

I've heard it argued that beaver ponds are best attacked with a short rod. Just as frequently I've heard good reasons for fishing these ponds with a long rod. The fact is that both have their moments. A long rod helps keep your backcast above the trees sometimes just as a short rod helps in tight quarters. I take along my favorite trout rod, which happens to be a nine-foot six-weight, and leave it at that.

A floating line will handle any and all tactics you choose to employ on virtually all beaver ponds. You will, however, want to cast long leaders much of the time, so carry spools of tippet material in 4X, 5X and perhaps even 6X.

Other than that, you are left only with choosing the appropriate attire. Drab clothing that blends with the surroundings is certainly an advantage in fishing beaver ponds, as such attire will help conceal your movements from the trout. Most of the time I wear an old pair of tennis shoes or a retired pair of hiking boots instead of waders. Over the top I usually opt for loose-fitting jeans or fatigue-style pants. Lastly, a pair of polarized glasses should be considered essential.

Flies For Fishing Beaver Ponds

The following list of dressings includes my favorite searching type patterns for beaver pond fishing. In addition to these patterns, carry some small Woolly Buggers in olive or black and a few Royal Wulffs or Royal Trudes for searching any tailwater sections where there is a reasonably heavy current and fairly deep water. Also add some kind of large caddis imitation to your fly boxes to imitate not only the large caddis that emerge in the evenings on some ponds, but also to mimic large night moths, which frequently get caught in the surface film of beaver ponds.

In addition, always carry a few terrestrial imitations, namely hoppers, ants and beetles. Specific pattern is not important, but usually smaller hoppers are more productive (sizes 8-10). I have found that simple fur ants are hard to beat, as are peacock-body beetles.

Some beaver ponds offer brown trout, which under the proper conditions can grow quite large.

Brook trout are the most common fare in many beaver ponds.

Lastly, keep a few streamers handy, especially if you fish in waters inhabited by larger brown and brook trout. Marabou Muddlers, with black, olive or white wings are productive, as are small Mickey Finns (especially on brook trout), sculpin patterns, Woolly Buggers and Zonkers.

Zug Bug (Cliff Zug)

Hook: *Wet fly or nymph, No. 8-14*
Tail: *Peacock sword*
Body: *Peacock herl*
Rib: *Fine gold oval tinsel, counterwrapped*
Wingcase: *Wood duck or mallard breast, tied in at front and cut off at mid-body*
Throat: *Brown hackle fibers*

Soft Hackle Zug Bug

Hook: *Wet fly or nymph, No. 8-12*
Tail: *Peacock sword*
Body: *Peacock herl*
Rib: *Fine gold oval, counterwrapped*
Collar: *Olive-dyed partridge*
Wingcase: *Wood duck breast*

Soft Hackle Hare's Ear

Hook: *Wet fly or nymph, No. 8-14*
Tail: *Partridge fibers*
Body: *Natural tan mottled rabbit fur*
Rib: *Fine gold oval*
Shellback: *Partridge breast*
Throat: *Partridge breast*

Carey Special

Hook: *Wet fly, No. 6-12*
Tail: *Fibers from feather of pheasant rump or partridge flank*

Body: *Peacock herl or dubbing (olive, brown, black and chartreuse are good colors)*
Collar: *Pheasant saddle for larger patterns, partridge flank or breast for smaller sizes*

Partridge & Orange Soft Hackle (Sylvester Nemes)

Hook: *Wet fly, No. 8-14*
Body: *Orange floss*
Collar: *Partridge breast*
Note: *Yellow or olive silk changes the dressing to Partridge & Yellow and Partridge & Green, respectively, both of which are equally effective on beaver ponds.*

Renegade

Hook: *Dry fly, No. 10-16*
Rear Hackle: *Brown*
Body: *Peacock herl*
Front Hackle: *White or cream*
Note: *A counterwrap of fine wire or thread through the body will extend the life of this or any other peacock-bodied pattern.*

Griffith's Gnat (George Griffith)

Hook: *Dry fly, No. 12-20*
Body: *Peacock herl (use the very fine herl from the eye of a peacock feather for the smallest hook sizes)*
Hackle: *Grizzly, palmered through body*

Gulper Special (Al Troth)

Hook: *Dry fly, No. 12-18*
Tail: *Grizzly hackle fibers*
Body: *Light olive dubbing*
Wing: *White sparkle yarn, tied as a post*
Hackle: *Grizzly, tied parachute style*

Chapter II

Sunfish

A redear sunfish—one of a half dozen different kinds of sunfish found in the Northwest.

"Yeah, I'd love to catch some redear sunfish—that would be a new one for me."

Thus began our relationship with the "secret pond" that Tim was describing to me with unbridled enthusiasm.

The word "secret," when used in context with Northwest fishing locales, always puts me on guard. In my experience, secret fishing spots, at least those arrived at by second-hand information, are usually only secrets to people living south of the Mason-Dixon Line. Still, Tim sounded convinced and confident and I was inclined to believe him as he explained that this secret pond contained one of only two redear sunfish populations in the state.

"Sounds like good info," I told Tim, "did you pry it out of one of the Fish & Game guys?"

"Better," Tim answered, "I ran into a guy through work who lives over there—he said he's caught redear up to a pound and generally has the pond to himself. He's a reliable source."

Pound-sized sunfish! Now that got my attention.

"When do we leave?"

Two days later we were bumping and banging through the sagebrush following one of those poor-excuse two-lane ruts they call roads out in central Oregon.

Just about the time I started questioning Tim's directions we topped out on a small rise a few yards away from some

five acres of prime farm pond. Unfortunately, three other trucks had beaten us to the few juniper-shaded parking spots. So maybe the pond was known to a few locals—that's to be expected.

The pond's glassy surface was gently dimpled time after time by soft sunfish rises, prompting us to string our rods in enough of a hurry to ensure that I would miss one of the guides in the process. (If you're like me, you never miss stringing a guide unless the fish are rising and you're in a hurry. You never discover the mistake until a critical cast during the peak of the rise.)

In any event, we were waddling shoreward with our tubes and flippers when another truck pulled up. Two more fishermen, but, like those already present, these newcomers were content to recline in a patio chair at the edge of the pond while drowning worms and draining six-packs.

Before entering the water, Timmy and I made a few exploratory casts from shore, hooking several five-inch largemouth. Five-inch bass being of limited entertainment value, we launched our tubes and began casting little sponge spiders along the reeds and other structures.

About that time our little adventure came unraveled, beginning with the arrival of about a third of the local high school's senior class, which had scheduled a "skip day" to the secret pond. They arrived complete with rubber raft, black lab, a few half-racks of Coors Light and plenty of scantily-clad gigglers.

Shortly thereafter, a pair of vans rattled up the road and off-loaded the entire population of rug-rats from a local kindergarten. Each kid came armed with a closed-face spinning reel and rod; each adult toted a carton of worms and a grimace that read, "this is a bad idea and there is no way in hell this day can turn out worth a damn."

The kindergarten, consisting of some 30 kids and six adults, filed into place along one bank and we were subsequently subjected to endless whining, bickering, bitching and griping. The children weren't too well behaved either.

After a fruitless half hour, one kid lucked into the dumbest baby bass in the pond. The resulting frenzy ended in eight or 10 tangled lines, about a dozen crying kids, two or three crying adults, and probably three or four ulcers and eventual career changes. The big loser turned out to be the pint-sized bass, which was first dangled by the lip at rod's end and bounced up and down like a bungee jumper, then flipped into the dust with which it was soon entirely coated, and finally pounced on by about five kids who mistook its last, dying flip-flop for some villainous attempt at escape. If that weren't enough, one of the adults, obviously lacking in kid-fishing etiquette, suggested that the fish was too small and should be thrown back into the pond. I probably needn't explain that this absurd act prompted another round of crying and whining, which in turn triggered more griping and bitching from the adults.

The high-school kids, meanwhile, had taken up the fine art of raft-stuffing, in which one attempts to determine the true carrying capacity of a two-man rubber raft. Any angler could have told the kids that a two-man raft holds exactly one full-sized man and a precious few selected tackle items, but they were determined to fit half a dozen boys and their respective dates into the boat. The resulting splashing, giggling and screaming prompted the thus-far well-behaved black lab to join in on the gaiety. From that point on, the dog spent the majority of his day in the water as any duck dog worth his pedigree is apt to do when relieved of the burden of discipline (i.e. out with the kids while dad's at work).

With all the commotion on that one side of the pond, Timmy and I figured we might find redears on the far side. We paddled in that direction.

There, on a shaded, grassy bank above the water, we spied a young couple whose faces were attached by interlocking tongues. They were oblivious to our presence, a fact that might be attributable to their obvious interest in one another or possibly to the foot-long glass bong at their side. This last article, which obviously held enough weed to make a small town high for a week, lent a certain charm (not to mention a certain aroma) to the whole scene.

Bear in mind now that everything we tolerated at "secret pond" that day would have been fine had big sunfish been forthcoming. As it turned out, the redear did indeed run about a pound—if you weighed about 12 of them together. They certainly were cute little guys, but I almost felt guilty of robbing the cradle.

Having thus conquered the mighty redear sunfish, we exited the pond, which harbored a larger population of splash-and-gigglers than big sunfish. I explained to Timmy what I thought of his "reliable sources," and to his credit, Timmy was halfway inclined to look the guy up and visit some sort of carnage upon him.

Just to punctuate the whole ordeal, Timmy and I were back in the valley lounging around the fly shop a few days later when a customer asked about any recent adventures in which we'd been involved. I mumbled something about redear sunfish in a little farm pond out east. Before I could finish mumbling, the guy said, "Oh, you mean 'secret pond'?"

I drilled Tim with a glare from the depths of hell. He just groaned.

Northwest Sunfish
Where to Find the Bluegill and its Relatives

A lot of anglers in the Northwest (and elsewhere) remember sunfish, especially bluegill, as their first fish, caught at an early age with dad's guidance. Indeed, many of us grow up around sunfish. But sooner or later we tend to graduate to trout, steelhead and salmon, forgetting how much fun can be had with a pond full of eager-to-please sunfish.

Bluegill are the most abundant, being found in waters all over the Northwest, from tiny farm ponds to sprawling reservoirs. Other sunfish, including the brilliantly-colored pumpkinseed, redear, and the green sunfish, are found in some places, although none are as widespread as the bluegill.

Washington's Seep Lakes, Twin Lakes in southern Idaho, Fern Ridge Reservoir near Eugene, Oregon—these are some of the traditional favorites for "bream" anglers. But the Northwest is home to so many sunfish waters that no

A pair of nice bluegill taken from a pond in southern Idaho.

A quiet evening of "bream" fishing on a deserted farm pond is hard to beat during the summer.

matter where you live, you should be able to find good fishing within a few minutes drive. Consult the fish and game agencies for information or dig up aerial photos of the local agricultural areas and pinpoint farm ponds on private property. Then go in search of permission to fish these places. Some of the best bream fishing is available on rarely fished farm ponds all over the Northwest.

Tactics For Sunfish

In most cases, the bream's abundance is due more to its ability to breed and reproduce uncontrollably than to its intelligence. That's the real beauty of sunfish: In addition to being abundant, they are generally pretty easy to catch. That's not to say they are always easy, but most of the time during the warm months, the bluegill and its relatives are generally cooperative.

The exception are big adult bluegill that have lived to a ripe old age of four or five years. For most of the year, these mature bluegill can be every bit as difficult and frustrating for anglers as a big spring-creek trout.

Whether you seek trophy bluegill or just a bunch of palm-sized sunfish to put a bend in the rod, your first concern is to find the fish. This task can be difficult at times. During summer, when water temperatures are comfortable for bream, the fish hang out in the shallows, always orienting to structure of some kind, including reeds, submerged or partially submerged branches and logs, pilings, docks, and other such items. Find good shallow-water structure and you're likely to hook all the bream you want.

Shallow, by sunfish standards, means anything from less than a foot to four or five feet. One of my favorite local bream ponds features ample shallow water decorated with a

smattering of reeds whose tops extend above the surface, a few tangled branches from fallen trees, some bottom weeds and some riparian vegetation. This pond represents ideal bream habitat.

During the spawning season (typically early summer) bluegill and other sunfish invade the shallows where they excavate beds on the bottom. In clear water, these beds are plainly visible: Look for shallow, light-colored depressions against the darker bottom. Generally you will find numerous beds in the same region. Even mature sunfish discard their native caution during the spawning season. Males are bent on defending the nest and grab or chase anything that approaches too close, including flies, jigs and other lures.

I'm not sure whether we are playing fair by fishing for bream on the spawning beds, but life generally isn't too fair for any of us, human or fish. Thus, at least at this point in my angling life, I'm not ready to chastise anyone for fishing over the spawning beds. For what it's worth, I allow myself to fish the spawning beds, but only to the extent that I'm not wading amongst the fish or hooking too many of them. I'll give myself six or eight fish and then move on to another area in hopes that I haven't disturbed the fish to any great extent.

Within a few days after hatching, baby bream are on their own. Mature bluegill seek places where they can feed in ideal water temperatures. During the balance of the summer, the fish suspend near structure in depths ranging from less than a foot up to more than 10 feet. As I am generally too lazy to worry about thermometers and fish-finders and the like, I simply look for good, fishy-looking cover. When I find brush-piles, reeds, boulders, weed beds, pilings, docks or any other similar structure, I stop and fish. I start high and fish my way down until I have covered all depths.

My favorite summertime tactic and the favorite of many fly anglers, is to find bream that will hit small poppers and sponge flies. Bluegill and green sunfish seem most prone to attacking surface flies.

During warm summer days—morning, afternoon, or evening—look for shallow-water cover, such as partially submerged reeds and brushpiles where big sunfish might be hiding. Cast a tiny popper or sponge bug into these places and allow the fly to sit still for at least 10 seconds. Big bluegill seem to relish the opportunity to swim up below a tiny popper and examine it in detail for what seems an eternity. As they do this, the fish generally like the fly to sit still. If a bluegill is inclined to take the fly, it will often do so when the fly is sitting perfectly still.

When you can no longer muster the discipline to leave the fly alone, begin a slow retrieve comprised of gentle twitches followed by pauses. The sunfish's reaction to your bug can run the gamut: Sometimes one or more fish will follow along gently plucking at the fly; other times a big bream will explode on the bug, throwing water all over the place in the manner of a bass. Still other times, the bug sends every bluegill running for cover. I can't explain why bream react in so many divergent ways to small poppers and sponge bugs, but I've learned to expect just about anything.

A few years ago, Tim Blount and I were fishing a narrow side-channel on a local slough when I found a willing bluegill holed up in a tangle of partially submerged tree branches. Again and again I cast a tiny cork-head popper to the fish and each time the fish did its best to inhale the fly. This went on for some 30 casts. The bluegill wanted that popper so bad he was driving himself into a frenzy. Bluegill being rather pathetically endowed in the mouth department, I finally tied on a size 12 Parachute Adams and hooked the fish.

It turned out to be a respectable hand-sized bull bluegill and despite its characteristic small mouth, it was entirely capable of eating my small popper. Why I couldn't hook it on some 30 tries with the size 10 popper is a question open to speculation, but I always keep a few small dry flies handy when I'm fishing poppers for bream.

As for specific poppers, I'm not too picky about color. I opt for small bugs in a variety of shapes. Those manufactured by the Gaines Company of Pennsylvania are perfect. Some of my favorite Gaines Company bream bugs include the Sneaky Pete, Pan Pop, Minnie Pop, Stopper Popper and Slippery Clyde. These panfish-sized surface bugs can be found at tackle shops and fly shops. If you can't find what you are looking for, ask if the store will special order for you or contact the Gaines Company (Box 35, Gaines, PA 16921) to find out where you can find a larger selection.

Recently I've been tying and fishing "mini-divers" for bream. The diver concept has been popularized by noted angler Larry Dahlberg, who fishes these alternately dry and wet bugs for bass, pike and other such creatures. I can attest to their effectiveness in that regard, but I hadn't considered the prospect of tying divers in sunfish sizes until I read Texan Jack Ellis' fine book titled "*The Sunfishes, A Fly Fishing Journey of Discovery.*"

The Dahlberg Diver is a deer hair contraption, looking something like a popper in construction. When you retrieve the diver, however, it darts under water. Continue stripping line and the fly stays under water. Stop stripping and the fly bobs back to the surface. What fish in its right mind could refuse a bug enlivened with such antics?

Ellis suggests in *Sunfishes* that mini-divers (he calls the patterns his Flathead Divers) will take small bass cruising in shallow water. So I tied some little divers—on size 10 hooks—and the first fish I caught was a six-inch bluegill. Consequently, I tied the pattern even more sparse to avoid short takes and have since found these flies to be fine bluegill patterns and fun bugs to fish.

No doubt, any sunfish that pounces on a popper, diver or sponge bug is worthy of pursuit. At times, however, simple trout dry flies work better. This is especially true of sunfish that rise for hatching insects during summer evenings.

A few years ago I was bass fishing on one of the lakes on the Oregon coast south of Reedsport. The bass had more or less settled any old scores that day by proving entirely elusive. Just as dusk settled over the lake, however, all hell broke loose in the form of a *Hexagenia* mayfly hatch. The *Hexagenia*, or giant yellow mayfly, is the leviathan of the mayfly world, spanning more than an inch in length, not including the tails.

What ensued was comical: Bream began rising all over the shallows, but the vast majority of the sunfish were not big enough to eat the huge mayflies. This I discovered right away and tied on a much smaller dry fly, a size 12 Elk Hair Caddis as I recall, and began ripping bluegill so fast and furiously that I almost feel guilty about it to this day.

Whatever the insect hatch in progress on a given evening, bluegill and other sunfishes often respond aggressively. Most of the time these rising bream are pretty easy marks, although I've seen a few evenings that I'd rather forget. After all, there is simply no profit to be had in admitting to your fellow fly fishers that you were outfoxed by a pond full of rising bluegill.

One trick that will tame some of those selective risers is to simply forget matching the hatch and throw a small wet fly on a floating line. A Partridge & Orange or similar Sylvester Nemes soft-hackle pattern usually does the trick, as might a soft-hackle Zug Bug or small Carey Special. Sometimes, in fact, a size 10 Muddler or similar streamer, allowed to sink a foot or two, will take a large bluegill hiding below a school of rising juvenile bream.

Even small sunfish are a lot of fun on a three- or four-weight rod.

Unfortunately I suppose, serious bream anglers must spend a fair amount of time casting sinking flies. During summer, the rules remain essentially the same: Look for appropriate structure in shallow water. Then work different levels until you hit fish. If a particular place fails to produce, move on.

Any number of fly types take sunfish below the surface. My favorites include soft-hackle Zug Bugs, rubber-leg bugs, small Woolly Buggers, and various soft-hackle flies. More important than the particular pattern is the style of retrieve you employ. Slow is the operative word most of the time. When I figured out that bream prefer to eat the fly as it is sinking or when it is moving very slowly, I began catching about three times as many fish as I had during my days of fast retrieves.

Certainly a fast retrieve can work wonders at times, but generally such tactics should be reserved for those times when the typical slow approach fails to produce.

Frequently, bluegill and other sunfish will take a fly as it sinks, either on the initial cast or during a pause in the retrieve. Such strikes can be difficult to detect—a problem that is only exacerbated by the sunfish's ability to inhale and then expel a fly faster than you can blink. The solution to this problem forms one of the important tactical considerations in fishing for bream: You must strive to maintain "contact" with the fly as it sinks.

If you employ a floating line (which will be most of the time) follow this procedure: After making a cast, immediately tighten the line to remove slack. Then watch that portion of the leader that is sinking below the surface. Any sudden pull or twitch and you should either pull on the line with your line hand or gently raise the rod tip. Although contrary to our trout-fishing upbringing where we are taught to raise the rod tip, I prefer to tug on the line when I see the leader twitch while leaving the rod tip at the water's surface.

This method requires a bit of discipline at first, since most of us are indeed accustomed to raising the rod tip when we detect a strike. However, a quick four- to six-inch tug of line with your line hand will allow you to set the hook very quickly. More importantly, the rod remains at the water's surface so that if you fail to hook the fish your fly remains near the same level in the water column.

Tim Blount casts small dry flies to bluegill
in this shallow bay.

A shallow slough like this one on Oregon's Willamette River offers perfect habitat for sunfish. Tim Blount caught three different kinds of sunfish without moving from this spot.

By carefully watching your leader you can maintain reasonable contact with the fly during the retrieve as well. Of course you will feel a strike that occurs as you strip line, but many strikes occur during the pause between strips. The method described above, used while you retrieve the fly, will help keep the fly at the appropriate depth if you miss a strike.

Often I will fish two flies simultaneously, spaced about two feet apart on the leader. This setup has resulted in many double hook-ups, especially with pumpkinseed sunfish and small bluegill. While fishing a two-fly rig on one of the small "seep" lakes in eastern Washington a few years ago, I had the opportunity to watch how sunfish react to the fly. The water was perfectly clear and I was fishing from atop a five-foot-high cliff. Below this cliff, in about four feet of water, I could plainly see my flies as they descended into a school of about 30 vividly colored little pumpkinseeds.

As the first fly reached the level of the fish, several would amble over to investigate. In a matter of seconds, usually before I had a chance to tease them with a twitch of the fly, one of the sunfish would inhale the fly. I would set the hook and in the ensuing commotion, the second fly would dance around following the path of the hooked sunfish. This second fly, jigging around the ball of sunfish, generally engaged several pumpkinseeds in a lively, albeit brief, chase until one of the fish grabbed it as well. The result was two hooked fish for the price of one.

The ability to watch sunfish react to your fly will go a long way toward helping you choose patterns and retrieves. Thus clear-water environments can prove a valuable part of the learning experience. Unfortunately, not all good bream waters feature clear water. In off-color waters, anglers must simply learn to fish appropriate habitat (e.g. structure) while employing methods and flies until the effective combination is discovered. Go through this process enough times and you develop a few standby patterns and retrieves: The same way that a trout angler fishing a tumbling mountain stream might instinctively reach for a size 12 Royal Wulff, a bream angler, with enough experience, will figure out a few highly reliable flies and techniques.

In any event, another deadly combination on bream is to dangle a wet fly some two feet below a small surface popper. Then fish the popper in the usual manner by casting, waiting, retrieving, waiting again. Although the popper might seem a bit suspicious to a fish watching from below, the trailing wet fly often proves irresistible. My favorite wet flies for this trick include any number of soft-hackle patterns (like the Partridge & Orange), soft-hackle Zug Bugs, Hare's Ear Nymphs, Humbugs, the Hazen Bluegill Bug, or just about any other wet fly that has earned your confidence.

Off-Season Sunfish

Summer is bluegill time. A hot, muggy day means a float tube and a farm pond full of bream. The fish are shallow and they are active. But what of the off-season—fall, winter and early spring—when the water is cool and our days afield are spent pursuing salmon, steelhead and trout?

The bream are still there, of course, and you can have them to yourself even on waters that have banks lined with anglers during the summer months. The fish still orient to structure. That fact never changes: Find good cover and you will find sunfish.

They hold much deeper, however, and might be sluggish and comparatively inactive given cold water. Still, the most difficult task lays in finding the fish, especially if they are holding 12 or 15 feet below the surface, orienting to some structural element (perhaps the bottom itself) that you cannot readily detect.

A sinking line, combined with a fair amount of patience, will lead you to sunfish in deep water. Otherwise, the same rules apply: Fish slow and fish structure. When you hook one bream, you can be reasonably certain others are nearby. Be especially mindful of the depth at which you hook a fish as they tend to congregate at a depth where the water temperature is most comfortable. To this end, use the countdown method with the sinking line.

The countdown method works as follows: First, determine the sink rate of your line (this information is printed on the box in which the line was packaged, if you don't have the box, visit your local fly shop and read a box from a similar line to find the sink rate). Then, after making a cast, count whatever number of seconds are required for the line

Sunfish often congregate around stands of reeds along the edges of ponds.

Sunfish often congregate around small, but visible cover. This snag was the most obvious place to fish since all sunfish orient strongly to structure.

to sink to the desired depth before beginning the retrieve. For example, if your line sinks at a rate of five inches per second and you wish to fish at 10 feet, you must count off 24 seconds before beginning the retrieve (24 seconds X 5 inches per second = 120 inches or 10 feet). Math not being one of my stronger points, I carry a card in my float tube or vest that tells me immediately how many seconds to count for a particular line to reach a given depth.

During periods of cold water, sunfish (like most fish), are most active at times and in places where they feel comfortable. Therefore, you can expect the best activity to occur during the warmest parts of the day and in parts of the pond, lake or slough where the water is warmest. Look for structure in sunlit areas, especially those places that are exposed to sun early in the day. If you fish reservoirs or sloughs, be sure to locate and fish old stream channels, as these places tend to attract bream.

In any case, summer will forever be the time of choice for bream fishing, but don't let the cool weather and cold water of the off-season lead you to believe that you can't catch fish then too. With a little persistence on the angler's part, sunfish can prove cooperative any time of year.

Flies For Sunfish

Naturally, surface bugs are the favorite choice for those times when bluegill or other sunfish are willing to rise. I enjoy fishing cork poppers in the smallest sizes, along with little "mini-divers." The poppers are available at most tackle stores. Make sure to buy those tied on size 10 hooks, size 8 at the largest. Another deadly surface bug is the Sponge Spider. These are easy to tie as all you need are the little preformed sponge bodies (available at many fly shops) and a turn or two of hackle. In addition to tying little deer-hair diving bugs, you can also tie hair poppers and sliders in miniature. In fact, tying these tiny poppers is something of an art form and is quite enjoyable when compared to the labor involved in creating bass-sized hair bugs.

In addition to the poppers and Sponge Spiders, you will want a selection of standard dry flies. These might include Parachute Adams', Elk Hair Caddis, Fur Ants, Griffith's Gnats and small Humpys. Along these same lines, standard trout nymphs and wet flies will generally prove effective

These effective "panfish poppers" are produced by the Gaines Company of Gaines, Pennsylvania.

when you fish subsurface for bream. Some of the top patterns include soft-hackle Hare's Ear Nymph and soft-hackle Zug Bug (see the "Crappie" chapter page 52, for dressings), Partridge & Orange, Pheasant Tail Nymph, Brassie, and small Girdle Bugs and Woolly Buggers. Damsel nymphs and scuds will catch bluegill on many ponds, especially in weedy areas. See "Chasing the Best Hatches" on page 30, for damsel nymph patterns; my favorite scud pattern is listed below.

Finally, bream anglers have developed many effective patterns specifically for their favorite waters. Many of these take bluegill and other sunfish just about anywhere. Listed below are a few patterns I have tried with good success, although countless other dressings are available as well. For a more complete listing of patterns, see *Flies for Bass & Panfish*, by Dick Stewart and Farrow Allen (Northland Press, Inc., 1992).

Hazen's Bluegill Bug (originated by John Hazen)
Hook: *2XL wet fly or nymph, No. 10-12*
Tail: *Black quill segment*
Body: *Black rabbit, dubbed rather loosely*
Head: *Red thread*

Marabou Brasshead
Hook: *2XL wet fly, No. 10-12*
Wing: *Marabou over a few strands of Krystal Flash*
Head: *Brass bead*
Colors: *White, yellow, olive, black*

Sheep Creek Special (originated by George Biggs)
Hook: *3XL nymph, No. 10-12*
Tail: *A few turns of brown hackle*

Body: *Medium olive chenille*
Wing: *Mallard flank (sparse)*
Note: George Biggs created this pattern for a trout reservoir on the Idaho/Nevada border, but it makes a fine sunfish bug as well.

Wet Madam-X
Hook: *Wet fly, No. 8-12*
Tail: *Deer hair (extension from shellback)*
Body: *Chenille—gray, white, olive or black*
Legs: *One pair of white rubber legs per side, protruding from chenille body*
Shellback: *Deer hair pulled over from rear and tied down at front*

Shewey's Super Scud
Hook: *2XL wet fly, No. 10-16*
Tail: *A short tuft of wood duck breast fibers*
Body: *Rabbit dubbing, loop dubbed using Krystal Flash*
Shellback: *Wood duck flank and a few strands of Krystal Flash*
Rib: *Fine gold or copper wire*
Colors: *Olive, olive-tan, creamy gray, tannish-orange*

Hum Bug (the Gaines Company)
Hook: *Wet fly, No. 6, 8, 10*
Body: *Chenille*
Back: *Chenille pulled over body*
Legs: *Rubber legs, tied in just behind head*
Head: *Chenille same color as back*
Colors: *White body/black back; yellow/green; yellow/black; white/red; chartreuse/black*

Chapter III

Largemouth Bass On Top

Float tubes are great for bass fishing because you can cast back toward the shoreline as Tim Blount is doing along this brushy bank on Coeur D'Alene Lake in Idaho.

My friend Brent Snow describes largemouth bass as "hyperactive carp," a description that I might find somewhat fitting if not for the fact that it is rather insulting to carp.

The truth is that I have little interest in a largemouth bass unless—and this is one big unless—the bass is in a mood to take poppers on the surface. The bass that hits a topwater bug is an entirely different character than the one that is dredged up with subsurface flies. In fact I'll go further in saying that the bass that whacks a popper is a major improvement over one taken deep.

Part of my aversion to subsurface largemouth fishing is that, unlike smallmouths, largemouth bass have a maddening tendency to pluck tentatively at subsurface offerings, only occasionally abandoning all caution to clobber any fly that ventures too near. Many fly anglers have devoted a great deal of time to figuring out the whimsical nature of subsurface bass fishing. I'm not one of them.

Also, it has been my experience that, in terms of fighting ability, the largemouth hardly compares to smallmouth bass and big bream. They fight hard, but only for a very short time. Nonetheless, my attitude towards largemouth bass turns a complete 180 where surface bugs are involved.

So, now that I have thoroughly angered the hard-core largemouth enthusiasts in my audience, the rest of us can get down to business on one the most exciting games in freshwater fly fishing: Watching a big bass, or even a little bass, explode on a popper, shattering the serenity of a quiet farm-pond evening.

Rather laboriously, you deliver a deer hair popper to a "bassy" looking area, perhaps a downed tree surrounded by reeds and lily pads. The popper lands with a watery "splat," sending rings of tiny waves dancing across the surface until they are absorbed by the reeds. You wait. All the rings have cleared and the bass bug just sits there, unassuming and wholly unprepared for the carnage to come. You twitch the fly once; then again. You wait a few seconds and then "pop" the bug wholeheartedly with a sudden strip of fly line—"gulup." Two more pops—"gulup, gulup." You are about to pop the bug again when some unseen fiend throws a bowling ball into the water where your fly used to be.

But wait. That's no bowling ball. A bass has just exploded on your bug, throwing water in every direction. You recover from the initial shock just in time to yank the bass out of the reeds before it can get too tangled. Good thing you chose that 10-pound Maxima for a tippet. For all its ferocity in trying to destroy your bass bug, the largemouth comes to the net quite quickly. But the damage is done: You're hooked on topwater bass fishing. How could any subsurface technique even compare to what you've just witnessed?

The ferocity with which a bass often attacks a popper leads me to think those bugs must really grate on the poor

Bass love heavy cover, especially during midday. In weedy places like this, anglers should fish poppers that include a wire or monofilament weed guard.

fish's nerves. Either that or largemouth bass simply lack any sense of subtlety where surface foods are concerned. Whatever the case, every fly angler should try this game of throwing surface bugs at largemouth bass. Granted, the Pacific Northwest is not exactly a largemouth bass capital, but we have plenty of productive waters teeming with bass from two to five pounds. Every once in a while, a fly angler in Oregon, Idaho or Washington will yard in a six- or eight-pound bass, but these are certainly the exception. Little matter, though, since even a two-pound bass smashing a popper is enough to double your heart rate.

In fact, largemouth bass waters are all over the place for those willing to study topo maps and then drive the backcountry roads looking for farm ponds. Often, the best fly-rod waters turn out to be the serene little ponds that require you to knock on the farmer's door some summer afternoon. In addition, many public-access waters, both natural lakes and reservoirs, feature excellent bass-fishing opportunities for fly anglers. Some of the top public bass waters in the Pacific Northwest are listed below, but bear in mind that equal if not better fishing can probably be found within a few miles of your home if you are willing to ask around out in the farm and ranch country. The waters listed below represent some of the major public bass waters in the Northwest—many smaller public-access ponds and lakes offer excellent prospects for those willing to search them out.

Oregon
Tenmile Lake (Coos County)
Tahkenitch Lake (Douglas County)
Siltcoos Lake (Lane County)
Lost Creek Reservoir (Jackson County)
Warm Springs Reservoir (Harney and Malheur Counties)
Willamette River Sloughs and Ponds
Fern Ridge Reservoir (Lane County)
Crane Prairie Reservoir (Deschutes County)
Columbia River Sloughs and Ponds
Bully Creek Reservoir (Malheur County)

Washington
Silver Lake (Cowlitz County)
Potholes Reservoir (Grant County)
Banks Lake (Grant County)
Eloika Lake (Spokane County)
Lacamas Lake (Clark County)
Kress Lake (Cowlitz County)
Sacajawea Lake (Cowlitz County)
Quincy Wildlife Area Lakes (Grant County)
Seep Lakes (Grant County)
Leland Lake (Jefferson County)
King County Lakes: Seattle-area residents will find numerous lakes and ponds in and around the Seattle area—check with the Department of Wildlife
Columbia River Sloughs and Ponds

Idaho
Chain Lakes and Lake Coeur d'Alene (Kootenai County)
Hayden Lake (Kootenai County)
Priest River (Bonner County)
Pend Oreille River (Bonner County)
Spokane River (Kootenai County)
Lake Pend Oreille (sloughs and backwaters) (Bonner County)
Conde Reservoir (Franklin County)
Twin Lakes (Franklin County)
C.J. Strike Reservoir and downstream on the Snake River where appropriate habitat is found
(sloughs and backwaters as well as adjacent ponds)
Paddock Reservoir (Washington County)

Wade fishing can be highly effective on small ponds. Here Tim Blount fishes a bassy-looking channel on a small Idaho farm pond.

Tim Blount lands a nice bass that couldn't resist a Dahlberg Diver.

Bass Bug Timing

In the Northwest, bass bugging begins during the spring—as early as March or as late as May depending on location and on spring weather. The first action generally coincides with what bass anglers traditionally refer to as the "pre-spawn period."

At this time, when water temperatures begin to rise into the mid- to high 50s, largemouth bass look to ambush prey in the shallows. Shortly thereafter (and again, the timing varies considerably from place to place and year to year) the male bass fans out a spawning bed and then seeks a mate. Within a day or two of laying eggs, the female bass moves off to deeper water, leaving the male to continuously fan the nest and then guard the fry.

During this period, bass—especially the males—are easy prey for anglers. Studies have shown, however, that largemouth require very little disturbance during the spawn to abandon their nest entirely. Moreover, the eggs require continuous fanning by the male to ensure a healthy brood. Yanking the male off the nest, which is easy to do this time of year because he is programmed to defend, deprives the eggs of being aerated.

The prudent choice, of course, is to avoid fishing for largemouth bass during the time they are spawning and attending the nest. This is easier said than done, however, because of the widely varying spawning times typical of Northwest bass. Bass in an eastern Washington lake might begin spawning a month or more before their brethren in a Willamette Valley pond one year, only to reverse the order another year. The precise timing of the spawn depends largely on water temperature, which in turn depends on weather patterns.

Because we cannot necessarily pin down precise spawning periods, bass anglers should avoid fishing over spawning bass when they are encountered. In other words, if you see a bass laying on a nest (a lighter colored patch against a darker bottom color), leave it alone. That's about the best we can do unless we elect to suspend spring bass fishing altogether, which would be ludicrous considering how much fun pre-spawn bass can provide.

Naturally, you can study a particular bass water so closely over a number of years to accurately predict the timing of the spawn. A few dedicated fly anglers can claim such knowledge of a few Northwest bass waters. But if you're like me, ardently pursuing all kinds of fly-angling challenges and sometimes going a year or more without casting a bass bug, you don't have the luxury of intimate knowledge on a particular lake.

One thing you can be certain of, however, is that as the height of summer approaches, bass bugging is at its best. During the warm or even hot days of July, August and September, fly anglers can enjoy some of the season's most relaxing and potentially most exciting bass bugging.

Largemouth bass thrive in waters ranging from 60 to 70 degrees. This temperature range is common on our Northwest bass waters during summer. When water temperatures climb above 70 degrees, bass move to cooler areas, including deeper water, shaded places, inlet areas and heavy cover.

In addition, hot weather prompts bass to feed most actively during early morning, evening and after dark. Quiet summer evenings on a bass pond can be special: The redwing blackbirds carry on endlessly, their shrill chattering as much a part of the pond as the bass themselves; bluegill dimple the surface everywhere; warblers flit nervously about in the willows and

Classic deer hair bass poppers crafted by expert tier Billy Munn of Bridgeport, Texas. These and numerous other dressings were introduced by Dave Whitlock.

a heron stalks deadly silent through shoreline reeds; dusk casts a golden-orange glow over the pond as a brace of wood ducks wheel effortlessly through the alders.

Amidst all this, the bass leave the confines of heavy cover and venture to the edges where they ambush whatever unlucky creature wanders too close. Perhaps that creature wandering too close will be your bass bug. If so, the serene surface explodes in the volcanic rise of a largemouth bass. Yard the bass out of the reeds and admire the simple, effective brutality of the beast—its spiny fins, perfectly camouflaged body and that gaping mouth that could and would swallow anything, including small mammals, reptiles, amphibians and unlucky birds.

For me at least, bass and dog-day summer evenings go together like barbecued salmon and a fine Northwest Riesling.

When autumn offers its orange leaves and cackling Vs of Canada geese, the bass are still shallow so long as water temperatures remain comfortable for them. But by this time I'm chasing upland birds, fishing steelhead and casting tiny dry flies on the Henry's Fork. Still, those bass of summer remain with me—the way they explode on a surface bug is unforgettable.

Bass Haunts

Successful bass-bugging begins, naturally, with a knowledge of where to find largemouths in shallow water. Any kind of vegetation is likely bass habitat and, assuming it is in the shallows, is probably good bass-bug water. Such "structure" includes flooded stumps and trees, lily pad fields, reeds and cattails, stickups, underwater moss and weed beds, overhanging willows and alders, pilings, boat docks and other like places. In the absence of vegetation or

wood structure, try bridge abutments, ledges, rocks, reefs and the like.

Always fish the shaded side of structure when given a choice. In fact, during periods of bright sunlight or very warm water, you may do well to concentrate entirely on areas of heavy shade. Often this translates to deep cover—places where a surface bug complete with weed guard excels.

The weed guard (a monofilament loop tied in to veil the hook point) is a critical ingredient in bass-bug fishing. This weed guard allows the bug to slide over potential snags without fouling—so long as the angler slides the bug gently over obstacles rather than trying to jerk the fly through.

When using a floating bug with a weed guard, cast into tiny openings in a lily pad field, into thick stands of reeds, over partially submerged trees and onto or over logs and stickups.

A float tube, of course, can help immensely in fishing heavy cover. The tube allows you to approach from the outside (lake) edge and cast back toward shore. Many bass haunts are virtually impossible to fish from any other location.

During morning and evening, bass move to the edges of cover where they wait in ambush, or prowl slowly about. Be sure to cover the edges thoroughly at these times and watch for telltale signs such as nervous water, splashes and moving reeds or lily pads.

In any event, perhaps the critical ingredient in bass-bugging is learning to fish systematically and with the expectation of finding bass in bassy-looking areas. Such expectations will help ensure that you fish thoroughly. A haphazard approach—a cast here, a cast there; hurried retrieves and run-about tactics—seems to produce less strikes than a methodical approach based on stealth and on thoroughly fishing each piece of likely looking cover.

Bass Bug Tactics

Timmy and I were tossing Dahlberg Divers into shallow, reed-studded water, allowing the bugs to sit still for a time and then retrieving them with a mixture of sharp pops and gentle twitches until they were a leader's length from our float tubes. The popping noise made when the Divers were yanked underwater seemed to carry across the lake: "Gullup," strip, strip, strip, pause; "gullup," strip, strip, pause.

A June thunderstorm rumbled off to the east, lending an eerie dark ivory cast to the Chain Lakes, which stretch along Idaho's Coeur d'Alene River and feed Coeur d'Alene Lake itself from the east. The acres of reeds glowed sublimely green; the water glowed vibrantly blue.

If nervousness attracted lightning, we would surely have been fried. As it was, the front seemed all too close and I've never relished being caught in a float tube a quarter mile from shore at the onset of an electrical storm: I tried it once on a high-country reservoir in southeast Idaho. Largely erroneous were subsequent reports of a hydroplaning float tuber skidding shoreward so fast that he nearly impaled himself on a barbed wire fence 20 yards up the bank.

Just about the time I was ready to rev up the fins for a mad dash to shore, some unseen gremlin tossed what had to be a cinder brick into the water right on top of Tim's bass bug mere feet from our tubes. The cinder brick turned out to be a bass, of course—a fact that we ascertained shortly after our respective heartbeats returned to some semblance of normalcy.

Simultaneously, a driving rainstorm let loose with all its fury, but we didn't really notice because Timmy was busy tussling with a largemouth that went about five pounds. This was the day's only bass. We had fished two hours without a touch, only to nail a big one just as the weather went to hell.

That little episode illustrated two important points: First, what's a little lightning between friends and second, predictability is not necessarily the largemouth's strong point. In fact, bass seem to thrive on unpredictability. Nowhere is this more evident than in fishing surface bugs. Sometimes bass prefer a dead-still fly; other times they pounce on a fly being skimmed quickly along the surface. Frequently, some retrieve in between these two extremes does the trick. On some occasions, every retrieve you try works; other times nothing draws a strike.

Due to their unpredictable nature, bass are best approached in a systematic manner based on two basic principles: 1. fish with stealth and 2. fish slowly and thoroughly.

As for the first principle, it should go without saying that the angler stands a much better chance if he or she can enter the largemouth's environment without the resident bass being the wiser. In other words, wade slowly and carefully; float tube or boat quietly. If you've never done so, take a few moments on your next outing to watch a heron as the bird hunts. I've always felt herons have a lot to teach human anglers: Emulate the bird's patience and stealth and you cannot help but improve your ability to sneak up on unsuspecting fish and slither into their world undetected.

So first train yourself to fish with stealth and patience, then concentrate on fishing methodically. I would venture to guess that most fly anglers fish bass bugs too fast most of the time. I've had the pleasure of watching some excellent bass anglers at work. They probe every foot of good cover. Other anglers are running willy-nilly around the lake, casting here and then over there and then back here again. The best bass anglers, meanwhile, quietly and methodically fish particular covers quite completely.

As the popularity of fly fishing for bass increased, more and more new surface bugs came about. These patterns are marketed by McKenzie Fly Tackle Company of Eugene, Oregon.

When I approach a lake, the first thing I look for, of course, is good bass cover. Once I decide on a place to start, I begin with several slow presentations. I cast the bug to a likely looking spot and then wait for a minute or so (or more likely 30 to 40 seconds since my natural impatience rarely lets me wait the full minute).

Long after all the ripples have cleared, I twitch the fly a couple of times, ever so gently. Then wait again, perhaps for 10 or 20 seconds, before resuming the twitches. After trying this ultra-slow retrieve several times, I move on to a more animated presentation consisting of "popping" a popper, diving a diver, or swimming a frog or mouse. Any number of techniques will work, but I usually start by allowing the bug to sit still until its ripples have cleared. Then I simply vary the cadence: two or three sharp strips of line, pause, twitch, twitch, pause, another sharp strip or two and so on. Bass often seem to smash a bug as it sits motionless following two or three sharp strips of line.

One of my favorite bugs, the Dahlberg Diver, fishes like a popper except that on the first hard strip, the fly dives underwater where it will remain as long as you continue to strip. Stop stripping line, and the Diver ascends to the surface, breaking the surface film with a gentle nudge. Bass often try to obliterate the Diver just after it returns to the surface.

Frogs and mice can be fished much like a standard popper, alternating pauses, strips and twitches. Another effective

Cork-head bass bugs have long been favorites of many anglers. These bugs are a few of the many styles and colors manufactured by the Gaines Company of Pennsylvania.

Tying spun-hair bass bugs has become an art form unto itself as illustrated by this deer-hair frog crafted by Skip Morris.

trick with frogs or mice (or just about any bass bug) is to cast the fly onto structure (logs, stumps, limbs, lily pads) above bassy-looking water and then strip the fly from there onto the water, where it lands with a splat. Allow the fly to sit still for awhile before beginning a retrieve. If the unmoving bug fails to entice a bass, try stripping immediately after you "jump" the bug onto the water.

No matter which bass-bug tactic you employ, keep the rod tip low to the water and pointed directly at the bug during the entire retrieve. This way you can manipulate the bug directly without worrying about slack line. Also, the direct connection between you and the fly will cut down dramatically on missed strikes, especially on those occasions when a bass rises the instant the bug lands on the water.

Tackle and Bugs For Largemouth Bass

Poppers, mice, frogs and divers cast about as well as live poultry on the end of a fly line and leader. To compensate for the air resistance of these large bugs, consider a stout graphite rod in the eight- to nine-foot range rated for a seven- or eight-weight line. Match the rod with a "bass bug taper" fly line. These specialty lines are designed with most of their weight in a heavy, rather short, front taper, thus allowing for reasonably easy casting with big bass bugs.

In addition, your leader should be heavy enough not only to turn the bug over on the cast, but to occasionally yank the fly through dense reeds and lily pads. Stiff monofilament

Dahlberg Divers, originated by Larry Dahlberg, have become a standard amongst bass-buggers.

seems to make the best bass-bug leaders. I use Maxima and Mason, both of which are stiff and capable of withstanding the kind of abuse that would send the typical fancy, high-priced, foo-foo fly-shop leaders screaming for mother after half a day on a bass pond.

A good bass bug leader spans six to eight feet (including tippet) and tapers down to 0X, 1X, 2X or 3X material, depending on the size of the fly (smaller bug, smaller tippet).

The floating fly line will do most of the work, but I carry a sink-tip around as well, just in case I need to try my desperation tactic: During the retrieve, the sink-tip line will pull a popper or frog underwater much like a diving bug. Stop stripping line, and the popper returns to the surface. Bass often take the fly just as it breaks through the surface film after a series of underwater strips.

Fly tiers have designed countless bass bugs over the years, ranging from the mundane to the ridiculous. Most have one thing in common: They will, at one time or another, take bass. While I won't go to the trouble of listing particular dressings, I will point you in the direction of a couple of good pattern books for bass bugs: *Flies for Bass & Panfish* by Dick Stewart and Farrow Allen (Northland Press, Inc., 1992); *Bass Flies*, by Dick Stewart (distributed by Northland Press, 1989); *Flies: The Best One Thousand*, by Randle Scott Stetzer (Frank Amato Publications, 1992).

One of the best all-around popping bugs for Northwest bass is a simple cork popper in a fairly small size (just large enough so that bluegill don't make a nuisance of themselves while you are trying for bass). Cork poppers are sold at some fly shops and at many all-tackle shops. Another deadly cork popper, introduced to me by John Harter of Lamson Reel Company, is the Sneaky Pete,

manufactured by the Gaines Company. I put them to the test on both largemouth and smallmouth and I'm rapidly beginning to understand why John considers them his top surface bug.

As a result of my initial enthusiasm over the Sneaky Pete, I've put in a lot of hours using other Gaines Company poppers. Among their other gems are the Dixie Devil, Bass King, Popping Mary, Pan Pop, Minnie Pop, Froggie and Fabulous Fred. If you fish in weedy environs, try the Weedless Willard, a popper featuring a built-in weed guard. Also, one of the new Gaines Company offerings, the Slippery Clyde, functions much like a Sneaky Pete but creates more surface disturbance. The Gaines Company offers all these popping bugs in a countless array of colors and several sizes.

Still another Gaines lure, the Trouble Maker, is actually an elongated surface plug meant for terminal tackle. Remove one of the treble hooks from a small-sized Trouble Maker, however, and you've got a deadly fly-rod bug. For information on where to obtain Gaines Company cork bugs, all of which are carefully and creatively hand-crafted, contact the company at Box 35, Gaines, Pennsylvania, 16921.

Incidentally, as you build your arsenal of bass bugs, include plenty of small bluegill sized poppers. I have often found these small bugs to entice strikes from bass that seem too shy to attack larger poppers.

Tim Blount and I have also put Dahlberg Divers to the test here in the Northwest with very favorable results. In addition, more and more foam poppers and frogs have been developed by bass anglers in recent years. Among these are some intriguing creations by noted Northwest tier Skip Morris. Whatever surface bugs you ultimately choose, however, remember to fish them with confidence.

Chapter IV

Chasing the Best Hatches

The author fishes over a February Capnidae stonefly hatch on a central Oregon river.

As months go, March and April offer little to write home about, save dreary weather and tax time. Luckily, however, we can always look forward to the March Brown mayfly hatch in the Willamette Valley during early spring—I just wish I could drag a few IRS guys with me and introduce them to deep-water wading.

That particular mayfly hatch, on the lower McKenzie and adjacent Willamette rivers near Eugene, is more or less solely responsible for dragging my four-year journalism program at the University of Oregon into a five-year affair: Those hallowed halls at U of O held little sway over me come March Brown time and as early as my sophomore year I'd learned to cut way back on classes during spring term to free up time for a decent education—an education on the river.

By the time my first senior year arrived, the reality of a fifth year at college had become entirely obvious. Hell, if the money hadn't run out, I might still be at U of O figuring out ways not to graduate while continuing my education on the McKenzie.

That's how impressive the March Brown hatch could be then and it hasn't dropped off much since.

I remember one week in particular when the McKenzie flowed about as low and clear as it is apt to in early April, when each day a low-slung, muggy veil of clouds cloaked the valley, interrupted during the afternoons by flirtatious bursts of sunlight—perfect mayfly weather. The March Browns

came off on schedule at about 2 p.m. each day. For the better part of an hour, big rainbows, along with a few native cutthroats, lined up in the shallows to devour mayflies.

My attendance record that week included one visit to one morning class (Political Science 201, which I did not visit again until the midterm exam—after all, poli sci 201 is about as intriguing as the television test pattern) and total desertion of my afternoon classes. Luckily, I never signed up for summer school as my presence in any class that time of year would have warranted a full psychological evaluation, if not a lobotomy: Summer was caddis time on the McKenzie.

In any case, by my second senior year I had perfected the art of scheduling classes around important hatches, the March Brown emergence being the most important. Unfortunately, I ran into a jam that spring: I needed an upper division literature class and the only one that would not interfere with two critical morning journalism courses happened to be a mid-afternoon gig titled, "Western American Literature."

What the hell. I had yet to meet a lit class I couldn't conquer, actual physical attendance notwithstanding. By some twisted sort of fate, the first meeting of Western Lit managed to arrive on one of those perfect mayfly days. Consequently I contemplated Western Lit from the comfort of a knee-deep riffle on the McKenzie.

With some reservation I dragged myself kicking and screaming to the second meeting of Western Lit. And I enjoyed it, thanks entirely to Professor Glen Love—one of those rare and special teachers whose efforts, despite their relative brevity, transcend your collegiate life and affect your entire life.

No wonder: Glen Love turned out to be a fly angler not to mention an old-time member of the McKenzie Fly Fishers—the original Federation of Fly Fishers club. Pretty soon he figured out that he'd seen my by-line in a fly fishing periodical or two. After that it was smooth sailing: I enjoyed Western Lit, but I didn't feel so guilty when the March Browns tempted me away from class a few times too many—Professor Love's class-attendance requirement notwithstanding.

I never discussed with Professor Love the reasons for my somewhat-too-frequent absences from class, but I think he knew. I think he understood as only another fly angler can. In the end I think he cut me a little slack—maybe not consciously, as he was fair and even-handed in matters that concerned his class, but on some cognitive level I think he made an allowance of sorts for the March Browns and the sway they held over me.

The Northwest's Top Hatches

Asked to name their favorite Northwest insect hatches, 10 anglers might list 10 different hatches. After all, we can fish over a number of top-notch hatches, from the tiny *Trico* (white-winged black) mayflies of the spring creeks to the giant salmonflies that emerge on famous freestone rivers like the Deschutes and upper Snake.

In short, we all have our favorites and this chapter discusses mine: the mahogany duns and *Tricos* of the Henry's Fork, the salmonfly and golden stonefly hatches, the damsel emergence on Crane Prairie Reservoir and Henry's Lake, the October caddis hatch on the Deschutes, the *Callibaetis* mayfly emergence of the alpine lakes, the spring emergence of large midges on the desert reservoirs, the winter hatch of little brown stoneflies, and, naturally, the March Browns of the lower McKenzie and Willamette rivers.

These hatches, of course, represent a mere sampling of the great insect emergences available on the Northwest's top trout waters. Another angler might choose any of numerous other hatches as favorites: green drakes, pale morning duns, black drakes on the Williamson, *Brachycentrus* caddis, *Baetis*

"March Brown weather" on the Lower McKenzie—warm, cloudy days during early spring generally produce the best hatches on the McKenzie and nearby Willamette rivers.

A fat little native rainbow from the McKenzie.

mayflies, etc. But those previously listed represent the hatches that motivate me to jump in the truck and at times drive some ridiculous distances. What follows is a hatch-by-hatch description of my favorites, focusing on technique, timing and patterns.

Winter Stoneflies: Central Oregon

By late January during most years, several streams in central Oregon host emergences of little brown stoneflies belonging to the family Capniidae. The hatch gains strength through February, usually peaking by month's end, before tapering off during March. This is a midday affair, with the emergence corresponding with the warmest part of the day.

Thus it follows that warm days generally feature stronger and longer-lasting emergences than cold days. These little stoneflies appear more-or-less jet black with smokey brownish black wings, which are folded flat over their back in the typical stonefly style when the bugs are at rest. Small as stoneflies go, the little winter stoneflies are imitated by hooks ranging from size 12 through size 18. Though the smaller specimens are more common, I almost always fish a size 12 or 14 in an effort to mimic the egg-laying females. These females, carrying a conspicuous cream-colored egg sack at the rear of their thorax, flutter over the water to deposit the eggs—an activity that generally gets the attention of trout.

During strong hatches, trout respond en masse to the winter stoneflies, especially in the larger pools and deep runs where trout tend to spend the winter months. Weaker hatches can produce equally good fishing, especially if preceded by several days of good hatch activity: The trout get used to seeing the bugs and are then on the lookout for them around midday even on cold afternoons when most of the hatch activity is short-lived.

In fact, Forrest Maxwell and I had one of our best days on the Middle Deschutes River on a cool February day at the tail end of a cold front. We found very few naturals on the water that day and yet caught trout consistently until about 4:30 p.m. The hatch had been strong up until that cold front had invaded central Oregon a week earlier, but the trout, even in the absence of any substantial numbers of stoneflies, were on the lookout for the little bugs.

These stoneflies offer fishable hatches on several central and southern Oregon rivers, although the hatch can be highly localized on some streams. Regardless, the opportunity to fish

"Bloodworms", as they are sometimes called, are actually the larval stage of a large species of Chironomid that is abundant in the reservoirs of the Great Basin country.

dry flies to rising trout in the dead of winter makes traveling around the sage country in January and February well worth the effort.

Any of several patterns will effectively mimic the little stoneflies. For flat water or reasonably flat water, I like a Floatin' Fool; for riffles or other choppy surfaces, a black Elk Hair Caddis or black Quigley Stonefly will float better.

Floatin' Fool

Hook: *Dry fly, No. 12-16*
Tail: *White poly yarn, clipped short (represents egg sack of female)*
Body: *Sparse peacock herl*
Wing: *White poly yarn, tied as post and clipped short*
Hackle: *Black, tied parachute style*

Black Quigley Stonefly (Bob Quigley)

Hook: *Dry fly, 2XL, No. 12-16*
Tail: *Black deer hair, short*
Butt: *Cream or white wool*
Hackle: *Black neck hackle, palmered or reverse palmered with fine wire rib*
Body: *Black rabbit fur, thin*
Wing: *Black deer hair with butt ends protruding at front to form head and antennae*
Hackle: *Black*

March Brown Mayflies:
McKenzie and Willamette Rivers

As early as mid-February, the first March Brown mayfly (*Rhithrogena morrisoni*) hatches begin on the lower McKenzie and adjacent Willamette rivers near Eugene, Oregon. During some years, the hatch won't begin until late February or even early March and on one occasion I found a smattering of March Brown duns on January 30. During a normal year, though, the hatch begins in earnest by late February.

An afternoon affair, the March Brown emergence coincides with the warmest part of the day, typically beginning sometime between 1 and 3 p.m. and lasting from 15 or 20 minutes to more than an hour. By mid- to late April, the hatch wanes, giving way to the late spring and summer caddis and stonefly hatches.

Every March Brown fanatic has his or her favorite patterns, although many anglers consider the Compara-dun and like patterns to be the standbys for the Willamette and McKenzie. My favorite is the Sparkle Dun popularized by Craig Mathews of West Yellowstone, Montana. Tied with a light tan body, the Sparkle Dun is identical to the standard Compara-dun in every way save the tail, which, in the former pattern, is made from sparkle yarn and is meant to mimic the trailing shuck of the emerging insect.

If the trout show any hesitation at eating the dun patterns, I'll attach a second fly: a soft-hackle wet fly designed to imitate the rising nymph. I attach this second fly by tying two feet of tippet to the hook bend of the dry fly and then attaching the wet fly to the end of this tippet section. After dead-drifting the offering past a rising trout, I apply just enough drag to allow the sunken fly to rise slowly to the surface. Trout often take the wet fly during its ascent to the surface.

For the most part, March Browns offer pretty straightforward fishing: Get a good drag-free drift with a dry fly and you're usually in business, especially on those cool, overcast days when the duns ride the water for many yards while drying their wings. My preference is to cast downstream and slightly across to the trout in the manner I would fish a spring-creek hatch. The downstream angle allows for precise fly placement and offers a fly-first drift to the fish.

March Brown Compara-dun

Hook: *Dry fly, No. 12-14*
Tail: *Deer hair or micro fibetts, divided (or use Z-lon for a trailing shuck, making the fly into a Sparkle Dun)*
Wing: *Fine natural brown deer hair*
Body: *Pale tan dubbing*

March Brown Soft Hackle

Hook: *Wet fly, No. 12-14*
Tail: *Short partridge fibers*
Body: *Light tan rabbit fur dubbed in claret silk*
Wing: *A few strands of tan Z-lon or sparkle yarn trailing over body*
Hackle: *Two turns of brown partridge or ruffed grouse hackle*

Early spring marks the beginning of Chironomid time on the desert reservoirs, but the weather that time of year can be brutal.

Salmonfly. Dave McNeese photo

Chironomids: Great Basin Reservoirs

The trout reservoirs of the Great Basin desert grow big trout for a simple reason: These waters are among the most fertile of cold-water environments.

Every stillwater trout food is represented, often in staggering numbers. One of my favorite reservoirs in Nevada is so loaded with big scuds that I've often quipped about using them as cocktail shrimp. Another of my favorites, this one in southern Idaho, features such astounding numbers of damsels that it's a wonder the trout eat anything else during the spring and summer.

Indeed while trout in many of these reservoirs can choose from ample supplies of everything from the scuds, damsels and mayfly nymphs to leeches, snails and water beetles, all, at one time or another during the year, feed heavily on Chironomids (midges). The desert reservoirs of the Great Basin harbor awesome densities of Chironomids, often rather large ones.

The best Chironomid activity generally occurs early in the year, especially during March, April and May. One particular Chironomid—the "bloodworm," as it is sometimes called—is responsible for the season's first dry-fly action on many of these waters. The larvae of these large midges are easily recognizable by their large size (1/4 to 1/2 inch) and reddish or red-and-peacock-green cast.

The adults, obviously, are rather large as well, looking something like a large mosquito. They drift quietly on the surface while drying their wings for flight, allowing trout the chance to eat adults along with the more easily captured pupae. In fact, it is the low air temperatures of springtime that cause the newly emerged adults to remain on the surface for a time instead of flying off instantly upon emergence as is the case during warmer months.

The super abundance of these midges means easy pickings for the trout. In many reservoirs, the large midges comprise all but a fraction of the trout's entire diet for weeks on end during winter and spring. Generally the larvae and pupae are preyed upon most heavily. But during mid-morning on some waters, late afternoon/evening on others, the emerging Chironomids bring trout to the surface.

It is these cool-weather, early-season midge hatches that offer some of the finest top-water fishing on the Great Basin reservoirs.

I generally opt for a three-fly rig when the trout are cruising along plucking Chironomid adults and pupae from the surface film. The lead fly and the first dropper are pupae patterns designed to hang in the surface film or sink very slowly; the top fly (second dropper) is a Griffith's Gnat or another adult pattern that will skate effortlessly on the water when I impart slight twitches and which will also serve as a strike indicator for the pupa patterns. Naturally, this three-fly setup requires a long tippet and I prefer to space the flies by about 18 inches.

Golden stonefly. Dave McNeese photo

Damsel nymph from Henry's Lake in Idaho.

If a breeze ripples the water's surface, cast so the line and leader will drift across the surface with the wind. "Wind-drifting" in this manner allows the flies to act naturally on the water, drifting slowly in the direction the wind is blowing and often fooling trout that refuse a retrieved fly. Still, when I employ this method, I usually begin a super-slow retrieve after a minute or so. This retrieve is comprised of a series of short, slow pulls followed by a pause of several seconds.

During cold, still weather, adult midges tend to be more numerous on the surface of the water. Unlike most moving-water Chironomid hatches, these early spring stillwater midge emergences lend themselves well to dry-fly fishing—a fact which is undoubtedly attributable to the amount of time the adult midges spend on the surface after escaping their pupal shucks. In short, since the trout have plenty of time to catch the adult midges, they will eat these winged Chironomids along with the pupae.

A Griffith's Gnat really shines at these times because it adequately mimics the adults and is easy to manipulate on the surface. You can slowly skate the Griffith's Gnat on the surface, imitating an adult midge trying to get airborne or one being blown over the surface, without ever drowning the fly.

At times, especially on warm days, trout concentrate on pupae at or near the surface. As previously discussed, the three-fly setup using two pupa imitations and a dry fly as a strike indicator will perform very well. More difficult are those times when trout key on the Chironomid larvae near the bottom.

Conventional wisdom tells us that midge larvae are largely unavailable to stillwater trout because the insects remain buried in the bottom debris until the emergence period. Indeed, my observations lead me to believe this is true much of the time. However, many of the Great Basin reservoirs offer exceptions: At times, mostly during winter and spring, larvae are heavily preyed upon.

Just a couple years ago I cleaned a pair of trout from a reservoir in southeast Oregon and found the trout to be completely stuffed with midge larvae—no wonder the fishing that March morning had been so slow. In any case, anglers should be prepared to mimic all three stages of the Chironomid's life—larvae, pupae and winged adult. Naturally, those occasions when trout look for adults offer the most intriguing midge fishing, this is quite common during spring.

Shewey's Bloodworm Larva
Hook: *2XL or 3XL wet fly, No. 10-14*
Tail: *Minute tuft of white Antron*
Body: *Three strands of red Flashabou mixed with one strand of green Flashabou, wrapped up hook shank*
Rib: *Fine copper wire, counterwrapped*
Head: *Fine peacock herl with a small tuft of white Antron protruding at front*

Shewey's Bloodworm Pupa
Hook: *2XL or 3XL dry fly, No. 10-14*
Tail: *Fluff from the base of a grizzly hackle*
Body: *Dark red-green dubbing*
Rib: *Fine copper wire*
Head: *For patterns fished at surface: ball of white closed-cell foam, which causes the fly to suspend in the surface film and a few turns of peacock. For patterns fished just under the surface: tuft of white Antron under peacock herl*

Shewey's Re-Vertical Midge Emerger
Hook: *Dry fly, No. 10-14 (Partridge No. L4A)*
Tail: *Minute tuft of white Antron*
Body: *Fine peacock herl, stripped until last three or four turns*
Rib: *Fine copper wire*
Hackle: *Very stiff, high-quality dry fly hackle, tied tight against eye of hook; 4-5 turns*

Griffith's Gnat (originated by George Griffith)
Hook: *Dry fly, No. 10-14*
Body: *Peacock herl*
Hackle: *Grizzly, palmered through body*
Note: *To make this fly durable, tie the hackle in at the rear, wind your thread to the front and tie in the peacock herl; wind the herl backward, then wind the hackle forward locking down the peacock herl in the process*

Salmonflies and Golden Stoneflies

The bugs alone are impressive: One to two inches long, vibrantly colored, covering the bushes to the point that willow branches and grass blades droop under the weight. More impressive is the rise of a trout to these huge stoneflies. At times the fish seem to abandon their native caution in an effort to pummel what obviously constitutes a fine meal.

No doubt the hatches of salmonflies (*Pteronarcys*) and big golden stoneflies (several genera) constitute one of fly fishing's most awesome spectacles. Consequently, the best of these hatches, which occur on rivers like the South Fork of the Snake and the Deschutes, attract many anglers each season, all of them drawn by the opportunity to rise big trout on giant dry flies.

Certainly there are times when trout don't seem to react to the big bugs. Such times generally arrive with the first days of the hatch, when the trout are only beginning to recognize that these giant floating objects can be eaten, and with the latter stages of the hatch, when trout are so gorged with stoneflies that they often pass them up in preference for smaller insects. Anytime in between, however, will likely find trout eager to grab these massive stoneflies.

Generally, salmonflies begin to hatch earlier in the year than the goldens. On some rivers, the golden stones begin their emergence toward the middle or end of the salmonfly hatch (which may last one to three weeks on most rivers). On other streams, the golden stoneflies do not appear until the salmonfly hatch has subsided. Typically, salmonflies hatch between mid-May and late June, depending on the specific stream. Also, the hatch tends to progress upstream as water temperatures reach optimal levels.

The nymphs of both types of stoneflies crawl to shore during the morning where they climb out of the water on rocks, vegetation, bridge abutments and other such objects. Once the nymph is out of the water, its exoskeleton splits down the back and the winged adult emerges. Then the adult must wait for its wings to dry before it can fly. During the afternoon, stoneflies leave the cover of shoreline foliage and begin their ovipositing flights over the river. On a good day, stoneflies fill the air, with dense columns of giant bugs extending a hundred feet or more into the air.

During the morning, trout hang just off the shore looking for stoneflies that have fallen from the trees. As the ovipositing flight ensues, however, even the fish living at mid-river are apt to rise for the adults These large flights of adult stoneflies can last until dusk during warm weather. Regardless, the best stonefly fishing generally will be found tight against the banks, especially where overhanging shrubbery and trees offer shade, protection and the promise of falling bugs for waiting trout.

The Deschutes River stonefly hatch generally begins in late May and runs through mid-June. Golden stones appear during the late stages of the salmonfly hatch. As with any river, timing can vary from year to year. On the Henry's Fork in Idaho, the timing of the salmonfly hatch is similar, although the golden stoneflies can emerge as late as early July. Meanwhile, the stonefly hatch on the South Fork of the Snake occurs from late June through mid- to late July. No doubt these three rivers offer some of the finest stonefly hatches in the Northwest. However, countless other streams, large and small, offer impressive hatches as well. I hiked into a remote little desert stream a few years ago in late May only to find one of the best salmonfly hatches I've ever encountered. So be alert to the possibility of stoneflies on most any of our freestone rivers during the early part of summer.

Always carry several types of adult stonefly imitations. If a trout refuses one pattern, switch to a different fly, which often entices a more willing rise. Refusals take several forms: Sometimes you catch the glint of sun off the trout's flank as it turns away a foot or six inches under your fly; other times you might see a slight bulge of water under the fly, indicating the trout changed its mind just inches before taking; just as common are trout that rise for the fly with no real intention of eating it—they bat the fly with their noses or flanks as if out of habit, but refuse to eat.

When any of those things happen, switch to a new pattern and one that is quite different from the fly that drew the refusal. I almost always begin with a Jughead, but upon a refusal I switch to any number of more sparsely dressed patterns: Norm Wood Special, Stimulator, Clark's

Freshly emerged damsels drying their wings. Note the olive coloration of the newly emerged insects as opposed to the blue or gray-blue color of the adults.

Stone, Bird's Stone, Lawson H.F. Stone or Sofa Pillow. (Granted, the old Sofa Pillow has lost its favor amongst anglers under the weight of the many new and fanciful patterns about these days, but I still catch a lot of trout on that fly.) In other words, I carry a pretty wide assortment of stonefly patterns. Most of the time, the Jughead does the trick. On those occasions when trout refuse the Jughead, however, I waste no time in showing them a new pattern.

During the latter stages of the hatch, when trout are stuffed with adult stoneflies, the fish sometimes allow numerous insects to drift by unmolested. Then, on the fifth, tenth or 20th fly, they rise, only to sit tight again as numerous bugs float overhead. This behavior on the trout's part requires anglers to fish with patience. Continue making good, quiet casts and sooner or later the trout will rise again.

In any event, the hatches of these giant stoneflies is a phenomenon that every fly angler should experience. Nothing in fly fishing can really match the spectacle, especially on blue-ribbon waters like the Henry's Fork, South Fork and Deschutes where impressive-sized trout rise for the giant bugs.

Jughead (originated by Betty Hoyt)
Hook: *2XL dry fly, No. 4-8*
Tail: *Short bunch of stacked deer hair*
Body: *Orange or bright yellow wool yarn*
Hackle: *Brown, clipped short and palmered through body*
Wing: *Deer hair or red squirrel tail*
Head: *Clipped deer hair*

Lawson's Henry's Fork Stonefly
(Originated by Mike Lawson)
Hook: *2XL or 3XL dry fly, No. 2-10*
Tail: *Elk hair, bleached and dyed yellow (golden stone) or natural dark elk hair (salmonfly)*
Body: *Poly dubbing or yarn, yellow or burnt orange*
Hackle: *Brown, clipped short and palmered through body*
Wing: *Natural elk hair*
Head and Collar: *Elk hair, tied reverse to form bullet-style head. bleached elk, dyed yellow for golden stone; natural dark brown elk with orange band of thread tying down collar for salmonfly. Clip collar short on bottom*

Sofa Pillow (originated by Pat Barnes)
Hook: *Long-shank dry fly, No. 4-8*
Tail: *Red quill section or red fox squirrel tail*
Body: *Red floss*
Wing: *Red fox squirrel tail*
Hackle: *Brown*

Clark's Stone (originated by Lee Clark)
Hook: *Long shank dry fly, No. 4-8*
Body: *Gold tinsel*
Wing: *Macramé yarn (rust or orange for salmonfly; gold for golden stone) as an underwing, then natural dark deer hair, unstacked, for wing*
Hackle: *Brown*

Bird's Stonefly (originated by Cal Bird)
Hook: *Long shank dry fly, No. 4-8*
Tail: *Two dark peccary bristles or moose hairs*
Body: *Dark orange floss with two or three sections of dark furnace hackle, clipped short*
Wing: *Natural brown bucktail or elk hock*

Tim Blount fishes the damsel emergence at Crane Prairie Reservoir.

This brown trout was fooled by a Gulper Special during a *Callibaetis* hatch on an Idaho lake.

Hackle: *Dark furnace wrapped in front of wing and clipped top and bottom*
Antennae: *Same as tail*

Stimulator (originated by Randall Kaufmann)

Hook: *Long-shank dry fly, No. 4-8*
Tail: *Natural dark elk or deer hair*
Body: *Yellow or burnt orange dubbing*
Hackle: *Grizzly or dark brown, palmered through body*
Rib: *Fine gold wire, counter-wrapped*
Wing: *Natural dark elk or deer*
Thorax: *Orange dubbing*
Collar: *Same as body hackle, wrapped through thorax*

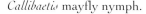

Callibaetis mayfly nymph.

Damselflies: Henry's Lake, Idaho and Crane Prairie Reservoir, Oregon

Damselfly hatches occur on stillwaters all over the West, but the hatches that occur on these two well-known waters are special in two ways: First they are tremendous hatches wherein phenomenal numbers of insects are typically present at the peak of the emergence and second, these hatches occur to the delight of some trophy-sized trout.

These days, a lot of anglers have that latter fact figured out. Both Henry's Lake and Crane Prairie Reservoir can get very crowded with anglers hoping to hook a few of those monster trout. Still, the damsel emergence on these waters is nothing short of awesome. In fact, both lakes frequently offer the chance to catch big trout on adult damsel patterns—something the unaccustomed angler will find impossible to forget.

On both lakes, the damsel emergence generally begins sometime in late June, peaking in early July. The damsels remain quite active on Crane Prairie through most of July. On a typical day on both lakes, the nymphs begin migrating mid-morning, looking for some object on which they can crawl from the water. By midday, the hatch is in full swing, with nymphs and freshly emerged adults clinging to vegetation, drowned trees, shoreline grasses and shrubs, your float tube and anything else on which they can escape the water; increasing numbers of adults take to the wing by mid-afternoon. The bright blue males are conspicuous compared to the pale dun colored females.

The newly hatched adults take quite some time to dry their wings and molt into the active, delicate-looking blue damsels that buzz over the lake's surface. I've

Callibaetis patterns.

watched nymphs crawl onto my float tube and then spend the better part of an hour completing the transformation.

These freshly emerged damsels are pale green in color with light yellowish tan or pale yellow-green wings. Any slight breeze catapults many of them into the water. Thus, windy days offer the best fishing with dry flies. Otherwise, you will do best to stick with nymph imitations. I fish three different nymph patterns: The first is a simple Marabou Damsel Nymph comprised entirely of olive marabou (with a wire rib). If trout prove uncooperative with the Marabou Damsel, I switch to my Wood Duck Damsel, which offers a somewhat more lifelike appearance. Finally, I tie floating damsels, which I employ when trout key on nymphs that are swimming (or hanging motionless) at or just under the surface.

Because most damsel activity occurs in shallow water, I usually opt for a floating line and a leader spanning some 14 to 18 feet in total length. A slow-sinking line is a good alternate choice, but anything heavier generally puts the flies in the weeds when you fish the shallow margins of Henry's Lake and Crane Prairie. Incidentally, I've often found that an ultra-slow retrieve outfishes any other method, especially when trout get difficult. Also, despite the fact that trout may be rising all over the place, I try to resist the urge to paddle toward every pod of rising trout. Instead, I try to remain more-or-less motionless in my tube and allow the fish to come to me.

Be prepared for some savage strikes by big fish. Often they grab the fly so hard and run so fast that you literally have no chance of keeping the fish out of the weeds. As a result, I rarely fish with the rod tip pointed directly at the fly as I would with many other types of stillwater flies. Instead, I cant the rod off to a slight angle from the line, rod tip in the water, so the rod will absorb some of the energy from those hard strikes. If the fish show a preference for gently sipping the flies, which they may do on any given day, I revert back to retrieving with the rod tip pointed directly at the fly so I can better feel subtle takes.

Marabou Damsel Nymph

Hook: *Wet fly or nymph, No. 8-12*
Tail: *Tuft of olive or tan-olive marabou fibers, nearly as long as hook shank*
Body: *Marabou fibers wrapped up hook shank*
Rib: *Fine gold wire*
Legs: *Small tuft of marabou tied in at front and splayed slightly to the sides on top of hook*

Shewey's Wood Duck Damsel

Hook: *Wet fly or nymph, 2XL, No. 8-12*
Tail: *Tuft of marabou from base of plume*
Body: *Thin marabou wrapped up shank, topped with about 15 wood duck fibers and 3-4 strands of pale olive Krystal Flash*
Rib: *Fine gold wire*
Thorax: *Marabou fibers wrapped on front 1/3 of shank*
Legs: *Olive-dyed partridge hackle pulled over thorax from behind*
Wingcase: *Lemon wood duck feather pulled over from rear of thorax*

Shewey's Damp Damsel Wiggle Nymph

Hook: *Standard length dry fly, No. 10-12 (abdomen is tied on a fine-wire shank with hook broken off)*
Tail: *A few strands of marabou fluff from base of quill*
Abdomen: *Fine olive dubbing topped with olive closed-cell foam and ribbed with fine gold wire*

Tricorythodes mayfly. Dave NcNeese photo

Trico patterns.

Thorax: *Marabou wrapped on shank, topped with an olive-dyed partridge hackle for legs*

Wingcase: *Fairly thick section of closed-cell foam pulled over the thorax*

Eyes: *Burnt mono or small plastic craft beads painted dark brown or black (optional)*

Note: Use a section of fine copper wire to attach the abdomen to the thorax: loop the wire through the eye of the shank on which is tied the abdomen and then tie this wire down on the front hook

Shewey's Emergent Damsel Cripple

Hook: *Dry fly, No. 12*

Body: *Pale olive elk or bucktail mixed with a few strands of chartreuse Krystal Flash, tied extended*

Post: *Butt ends from body, tied forward and folded back*

Wings: *A few strands of pearl or lime Krystal Flash or Z-lon, splayed and tied delta style*

Hackle: *2-3 turns of watery dun tied parachute style*

Shewey's Adult Damsel

Hook: *Dry fly, No. 12*

Body: *Bright blue bucktail or elk, tied extended (thin) with black thread*

Wing Post: *Butt ends from body, tied forward and pulled back*

Wings: *Grizzly hackle tips or pearl Krystal Flash*

Hackle: *Dun or grizzly, 3-4 turns parachute style*

Callibaetis Mayflies:
High Lakes Throughout the West

You're somewhere deep in the Rockies or in the high Cascades on a small alpine lake that you have all to yourself; trout begin rising during the afternoon, only a few at first, but soon you notice increasing numbers of medium-sized speckled-wing mayflies until, after awhile, they dominate the lake's surface and drive the trout into a feeding frenzy. You choose a like imitation, which needn't be too precise, and begin hooking strikingly marked alpine trout, which smash the fly as it sits quietly on the surface.

These are the *Callibaetis* mayflies, or "speckled-wing duns." They are the dominant stillwater mayfly on Western trout lakes and are especially prevalent in the high lakes of the Western mountains. Their hatches, which begin during the summer and last through early to mid-autumn, offer some of the best surface action to be found on the high-altitude lakes of Oregon, Washington and Idaho (not to mention the other Western states).

The *Callibaetis* duns are unmistakable with their characteristic mottled wings and tannish or grayish bodies. A size 12 or 14 pattern will mimic the first hatches perfectly, but because two or more broods of these mayflies hatch each year, the later specimens will be smaller, sometimes down to size 18s and commonly a size 16. The spinners, which usually appear prior to the hatch itself, can be of significance as well when they begin mating, laying eggs and falling spent in the shallows. Any time you approach a high-mountain lake between mid-morning and mid-afternoon be on the lookout for swarms of these *Callibaetis* spinners, the individuals dancing up and down above the water's surface.

Hatches and spinner falls present uncomplicated fishing. During any strong *Callibaetis* emergence, trout turn toward the surface as soon as sufficient numbers of duns are present. When you see the first few duns, however, consider fishing a *Callibaetis* nymph near the bottom in fairly shallow water. The nymphs are excellent and animated swimmers and tend to become quite active as hatch time nears. I like to fish two nymph patterns on a floating line and a long, light leader. I allow the flies, which are lightly weighted, to sink to the bottom and then I begin an active retrieve comprised of short bursts, brief pauses and a few slow pulls.

When I see lots of duns on the water and lots of trout rising for them, I switch to dry flies. A Parachute Adams or Gulper Special works well most of the time. Selective trout sometimes respond better to a Sparkle Dun or Compara-dun. Often a sparsely dressed soft-hackle emerger will prove deadly when fished just inches below the surface, especially where difficult trout are involved.

During the spinner fall, the same Gulper Special or Parachute Adams often suffices when non-selective alpine trout are the fare. When trout act fussy, however, I switch to a *Callibaetis* Krystal Spinner, which has proven to be my best pattern for these spinner falls.

The *Callibaetis* mayflies are so prolific and predictable on high lakes that their emergence is well worth pursuing—especially considering the majestic scenic beauty of our alpine lake basins. In Oregon and Washington, hatches can begin as early as May in the lower reaches of the wilderness areas, but July, August and September are peak months. At the higher elevations of the Rocky Mountains, peak activity begins in mid- to late July and continues through August and most of September.

Callibaetis Gulper Special (originated by Al Troth)
Hook: *Dry fly, No. 12-18*
Tails: *Hackle fibers or micro fibetts, divided if desired*
Body: *Pale olive-tan or gray-tan dubbing*
Wing: *Gray or tan poly yarn, short*
Hackle: *Grizzly or grizzly-watery dun mixed, parachute style*

Parachute Adams
Hook: *Dry fly, No. 12-18*
Tail: *Mix of brown and grizzly hackle fibers*
Body: *Light gray or tan*
Wing: *White calf body hair, poly yarn or similar*
Hackle: *Grizzly brown mixed, parachute style*

Shewey's Western *Callibaetis* Nymph
Hook: *Nymph or sedge, No. 12-16*
Tails: *Widgeon flank fibers, short*
Body: *Hen pheasant fibers or tannish marabou blood quill fiber tips, wound up shank*
Wingcase: *Medium tan partridge or ruffed grouse pulled over thorax*
Thorax: *Tan ostrich herl or sun-bleached bronze peacock herl*
Legs: *Partridge fibers*

Pheasant Tail Nymph
Hook: *Nymph or 2XL wet fly, No. 12-16*
Tail: *Pheasant tail fibers*
Body: *Pheasant tail fibers wrapped up shank*
Rib: *Fine copper wire, counterwrapped*
Wingcase: *Pheasant tail fibers*
Thorax: *Peacock herl*
Legs: *Tips from fibers used to form wingcase, folded back*

Adult damsels. Crane Prairie Reservoir, Oregon.

Mercer's *Callibaetis* Nymph
(originated by Mike Mercer)

Hook: *2XL nymph, No. 12-18*
Tail: *Three gray ostrich or rhea fiber tips*
Abdomen: *Creamy-olive dubbing*
Rib: *Pearl Krystal Flash*
Gills: *Sparse gray marabou on each side, tied-in in front of abdomen*
Thorax: *Same as abdomen*
Wingcase: *Dark turkey tail, coated with epoxy*
Legs: *A few wood duck flank fibers or grouse fibers, tied in at each side*
Head: *One turn of dubbing*

Callibaetis Krystal Spinner (John Shewey)

Hook: *Dry fly, No. 12-16*
Tails: *Micro fibetts or grizzly hackle fibers, divided*
Body: *Pale gray dubbing*
Wings: *4-6 strands of pearl Krystal Flash, tied 3/4 spent*
Hackle: *Mix of dun and grizzly, wrapped through wings and clipped flush below*

Callibaetis Sparkle Dun (Craig Mathews)

Hook: *Dry fly, No. 12-16*
Tail: *Tan Z-lon or sparkle yarn*
Body: *Pale tan dubbing*
Wing: *Fine deer hair, tied Compara-dun style*
Note: Compara-dun is tied same way but with hackle fiber tails

Callibaetis Soft-Hackle

Hook: *Wet fly, No. 12-16*
Tails: *Partridge fibers, short*
Body: *Light tan sparkle dubbing, picked out near front*
Hackle: *Two turns of tan partridge hackle*

Tricos (White-Winged Black Mayflies):
Henry's Fork, Snake River, Idaho

A strong hatch of *Tricorythodes* ("*Trico*") mayflies forms a wondrous sight: It begins with swarms of tiny white-winged mayflies dancing above the shallows, the entire mass billowed about by the slightest of air currents, its shape constantly changing, but always maintaining a sort of unity. Backlit by soft hues of early morning sunlight, these swarms descend on the river. They are comprised entirely of male "white-winged black mayflies" that by and large hatched the previous night.

Soon, however, the emergence begins in earnest, quietly at first and usually accompanied by a few tentative rises by trout anticipating things to come. Quickly the hatch gains momentum as more and more female *Tricos* hatch and then join the swarms of males where mating occurs. Even before the hatch has reached its zenith, the first spinners fall spent to the water after completing the act of mating and laying eggs. Thus what started as a hatch soon becomes both hatch and spinner fall.

By now trout have taken up feeding stations, where they rise steadily and methodically, almost greedily at times. For upwards of an hour, sometimes more, you cast size 18-22 imitations to particular trout until the *Tricos* finally disappear. Always, when it is over, you wish the *Trico* activity could have lasted another hour or so.

The quiet sections of the Henry's Fork offer impressive hatches of *Tricos* during August, when the action can begin as early as 8 a.m. or as late as 10:30, depending on the weather. Silver Creek, Idaho's other famous spring creek, hosts an impressive hatch as well, this one beginning during mid-July.

Given their minute size and the density of their hatches/spinner falls, *Tricos* can make for difficult fishing. One important tactical adjustment I made several years ago was to simply stay out of the water until the hatch is going strong and the trout are rising steadily and confidently. I don't bother stalking those first few rising trout and instead wait until many fish are working the surface.

In addition, I always carry a few ant or beetle imitations during the *Trico* hatch: Sometimes, when I'm having difficulty bringing trout to a tiny mayfly pattern, I find success with a small terrestrial pattern. Perhaps some fish start looking to the surface with all the mayflies about, but would still prefer to eat an ant or beetle, both of which spring-creek trout seem to relish.

All the tactics that make for successful fishing on the flat waters of our Western spring creeks are applicable to the *Trico* hatch: Downstream slack-line cast, precise fly placement, correct timing of the rise, etc. A read of my book *Mastering the Spring Creeks* (Frank Amato Publications) will help prepare you for the spring-creek experience.

Shewey's *Trico* Hackle Spinner

Hook: *Dry fly, No. 18-22*
Tails: *Three white hackle fibers, splayed and rather long*
Body: *Rear third white tying thread, front two-thirds black mole fur, dubbed*
Hackle: *White, wrapped through black mole fur, clipped flush below and V-clipped above*
Note: Hackle is wrapped through body in about 4-5 turns, each slightly spaced rather than tight against one another in the fashion of a typical dry fly

Shewey's *Trico* Antron Spinner-Dun

Hook: *Dry fly, No. 18-22*
Tails: *Three white hackle fibers, tied fairly short*
Body: *Black or medium olive*
Wing: *Fine white Antron or similar, tied Compara-dun style (or substitute CDC fibers)*

Mahogany Duns:
Henry's Fork, Snake River, Idaho

The mahogany dun (*Paraleptophlebia bicornuta*) emerges late in the season on the flat-water sections of the Henry's Fork, especially Harriman Park. Peak hatches occur during the month of September, with duns typically appearing mid-morning.

Like many mayfly hatches, the mahogany dun emergence is always bolstered by inclement weather. In fact, I've enjoyed some of the best mahogany dun hatches during rainy, blustery, cool days.

Thanks to the timing of the hatch (September) anglers can find plenty of elbow room on the Harriman Section ("Railroad Ranch") of the Henry's Fork. Such is not always the case earlier in the year when the Henry's Fork hosts its popular hatches of green drakes and pale morning duns.

Moreover, during a strong emergence, the mahogany duns can hatch for a period of three or four hours. During this time they hatch somewhat sporadically, never building into a dense blanket hatch like those associated with the little blue-winged olives that hatch later in the afternoon during September. Instead, mahogany duns emerge as if they're in no particular hurry: a few here and a few there, then a sustained wave of duns for a little while, then back to a few individuals scattered about and maybe back to another wave or two.

Because the duns emerge rather sporadically, trout must peruse a wider feeding lane than if they were feeding on a blanket hatch of blue-winged olives or pale morning duns. This behavior on the trout's part allows for less concern over precise casting accuracy on the angler's part. Moreover, mahogany duns tend to ride the water for quite some time while drying their wings, thus allowing trout ample opportunity to eat the adults rather than concentrating solely on emergers.

Still, I have seen trout feed selectively on emergers at the surface while ignoring fully winged duns but I have yet to see the reverse: selective feeding on duns to the exclusion of emergers. Consequently, I generally fish a floating emerger pattern.

A number of years ago I was camping on the Henry's Fork for a week during September. The first day greeted me with a strong mahogany dun hatch and I discovered immediately that I had somehow left my box of like imitations at home. Luckily I had packed a few materials and tying tools, so I returned to camp to see what I could whip up to match the mahogany duns. Since I had only a precious few materials to choose from, I created a very simple and somewhat ridiculous-looking mahogany dun emerger pattern.

The fly worked just fine, fooling quite a few fish that trip. Since that time, my Mahogany Dun Emerger has become my standard pattern for this wonderful mayfly hatch on the Henry's Fork. Other good choices include the Mahogany Dun Cripple Emerger and Craig Mathew's Sparkle Dun tied with a mahogany-colored body. Prior to the time when I whipped up those simple little emerger patterns at my campsite on the river, I used Compara-duns and quill-wing no-hackle patterns. Both are fine patterns when trout are eating duns. All these patterns should be tied on size 16 hooks (occasionally I've seen Mahogany Duns suited to imitation with size 18 hooks).

In any event, the mahogany duns are beautiful little mayflies and they emerge during the most vibrant and colorful time of year on the Henry's Fork. No doubt the green drakes and PMD's will always draw the most attention on the flat-water sections of the Henry's Fork, but every serious fly angler deserves, at least once, to visit this splendid river during September.

Shewey's Mahogany Dun Emerger
Hook: *Dry fly, No. 16*
Tail: *Brown Z-lon or sparkle dubbing tied as trailing shuck*
Body: *Brown dubbing*
Wing: *Same as tail, tied Compara-dun style and slightly undersized*

Mahogany Dun Cripple Emerger
Hook: *Dry fly, No. 16*
Tail: *Light brown Z-lon or sparkle dubbing as a trailing shuck*

Angler plays a big trout on a desert reservoir

Body: *Brown dubbing*
Wings: *Gray Z-lon or similar, tied Compara-dun style and then divided in half and splayed back and to the sides (delta style)*
Hackle: *Two turns of pale watery dun, clipped below*

Mahogany Sparkle Dun
Hook: *Dry fly, No. 16*
Tail: *Tan sparkle yarn or Z-lon*
Body: *Mahogany-brown dubbing*
Wing: *Fine deer hair, tied Compara-dun style*

October Caddis:
Deschutes River, Oregon

If you hit it right, the October caddis hatch on Oregon's Deschutes River is as good or better than any such hatch on any river in the West: Well after sunset, during the last hour of October light, the giant caddis appear in hordes, dominating the scene so suddenly and quickly that you wonder how you managed not to notice the first few bugs. They are everywhere: in the air, on the water, on the bushes, in your ears, eyes and mouth. Fish are rising: Trout feast on the huge caddis; whitefish, disconcerted by all the action, rise for the big bugs but I doubt that any but the largest whitey can actually ingest into its puny mouth an adult October caddis. Here and there a steelhead swirls for a giant caddis. Even the squawfish work the surface—a fact which seems something of a contradiction in terms. I've caught countless big squawfish on dry flies during heavy Deschutes River October caddis hatches.

But that is only if you hit it just right. More often, the hatch is a fleeting affair comprised of a few caddis here and a few caddis there, prompting some surface activity, but by and large overshadowed by simultaneous emergences of small caddisflies. Still, during late September, October and often into early or mid-November, the chance exists that you will be at the right spot on the river during one of those magical October caddis hatches when the bugs appear in voluminous hordes.

Some confusion exists in the fly angling world as to just how the fall caddis emergence occurs. Some writers and anglers suggest that the pupae crawl ashore to emerge (on rocks, limbs, grass, etc.); others assume that the big pupae swim to the surface and emerge astream. My own observations lead me to believe that perhaps both strategies are employed simultaneously, with some pupae swimming to shore and crawling out, while others indeed emerge through the surface film. I base this conclusion on the success I have had fishing pupae patterns just under the surface, where trout attack the fly with a vengeance as if they are quite used to doing so.

By far the most successful technique I have found for fishing the typical October caddis hatch is to employ a two-fly rig featuring a high-floating dry (a Jughead or Bucktail Caddis) as a dropper about two feet above a pupa pattern that is fished wet. The adult mimics the egg-laying adult and as such can be skated and skittered on the surface by applying rod tension. Each time you twitch the dry fly, you enliven the pupa pattern, causing it to suddenly lift toward the surface. Vicious strikes on both the dry and the wet fly are the norm.

If I am casting to particular trout, I offer a dead-drift presentation first. If four or five such drifts fail, I then offer the twitched or skated fly.

In any event, the October caddis (also known as fall caddis and giant orange caddis) offers short-lived evening hatches, so take advantage when you encounter one. The hatch occurs on virtually all sections of the river, from the lower sections above the confluence with the Columbia (where I've seen the best hatches), all the way up to the Warm Springs area. A heavy hatch one evening does not assure you of a heavy emergence on subsequent evenings and sometimes you can spend an entire autumn looking for but not finding a heavy hatch of fall caddis on the Deschutes. Still, when it is good, the October caddis hatch is nothing short of captivating.

Jughead Caddis

Hook: *2XL dry fly, No. 6-8*
Tail: *Short bunch of deer hair*
Body: *Orange wool yarn*
Hackle: *Brown, clipped and palmered through body*
Wing/Head: *Deer hair, spun and clipped to form fairly robust Muddler-style head*

October Caddis

Hook: *2XL dry fly, No. 6-8*
Tail: *Short bunch of deer, elk or moose (to provide flotation support)*
Body: *Orange wool yarn*
Hackle: *Brown, palmered or reverse palmered and ribbed with fine wire*
Wing: *Natural deer or elk, butt ends left to form head*
Collar: *Mix of brown and grizzly hackle wrapped over wing at tie-down point*

Shewey's October Caddis Pupa

Hook: *Wet fly or sedge hook, No. 6-8 (if light wire hook is used, tie a short length of fine lead wire along hook shank)*
Tail: *Partridge fibers, very short*
Body: *Pale tan-orange dubbing, loosely loop dubbed with orange Krystal Flash*
Wings: *Brown partridge hackle tips, one per side, tied low*
Hackle: *Two turns of brown partridge or ruffed grouse hackle*
Head: *Black ostrich herl*

This big rainbow fell for an emergent cripple during the mahogany dun hatch on the Henry's Fork of the Snake River in Idaho.

Chapter V

Golden Trout and Grayling

Grayling over a foot long are considered prize catches in the alpine country.

"I'm never going to see a moose in the wild," complained Dee as the truck bumped and banged along a busted up, potholed excuse for a road leading to one of the more remote trailheads in Wyoming's Wind River Mountains.

"Look Dee, I grew up in moose country and I promise you we'll see a moose in here somewhere—this is perfect country for them," I assured her.

Incredibly, we snailed along some 12 miles of very ugly road that paralleled some very pretty moose country without ever catching so much as a glimpse of one of the beasts. By the time we'd reached the trailhead, I had forgotten about the moose, my mind instead racing ahead to the thought of golden trout in some tiny alpine lakes about eight miles up in the Winds.

Dee hadn't forgotten about her moose. Some women like cute little teddy bears; others like moose I guess—I should never have bought her that cute little fuzzy stuffed moose toy from one of the churn-your-stomach West Yellowstone gift shops, but I felt pretty bad about leaving her behind when I ran off to the Federation of Fly Fisher's Conclave one year.

"I told you we'd never see a moose," she continued, "I'm just bad luck when it comes to seeing stuff like that."

This from a women who had once mentioned never having seen a bear in the wild only to have one amble across the road in broad daylight two minutes later; this from a woman who complained about never seeing an elk up close only to

have a six-point bull jump up from his bed and nearly run us down in his haste to leave the premises.

With golden trout on the brain, I didn't much care about the moose anymore. "Look Dee, we can't help but see a moose in country like this, so don't worry about it."

"I'll bet you ten bucks we don't see a moose," she retorted. Given the kind of country we were in—perfect moose country—I took the bet and then prompted Dee to don the packs and hit the trail—the sun was an hour up and we had a long, hard hike ahead of us.

As it turned out, long and hard barely described the punishment doled out on us by that rugged trek high into the Winds. Any sane person would have taken two or three days to make the trek. I've never been accused of being too sane, nor of being overwhelmingly endowed with common sense, so we elected to make the journey in a single day. The first six miles were brutal and exhausting, with steepness increasing exponentially. After that, it got difficult.

Finally we reached our little lake, nestled exquisitely in a small glaciated pocket amongst several rocky crags. Thunderheads were assembling for the typical afternoon onslaught of fireworks to be expected during August, so we strung the rods and began fishing immediately. Golden trout were both abundant and willing. After an hour and a half of wonderful fishing, Dee looked first at the sky and then at her watch and said we'd better get the hell out of there.

Luckily she brings the common sense to the table. Given my druthers, I'd have probably fished till dusk and then killed myself trying to descend steep talus slides after dark. With a last longing look at the emerald-colored lake, the meadow alive with a rainbow of wildflowers, and the snow-capped crags, we hauled off over the first of several nasty escarpments and picked our way some 2,000 feet down to the next basin.

With six miles left to go and late afternoon rapidly yielding to evening, we picked up the pace, hoping we wouldn't need to do too much night-hiking to reach the trailhead. A small herd of elk trampled off through woods so near that we could smell them. Only upon reaching the first of three big stream-fed meadows did we slow enough to look around. I figured we would find Dee's moose in one of those lush meadows—perhaps close enough to photograph. I was amazed that the first meadow contained not a whisper of wildlife.

By the time we reached the second meadow, the light was failing to the point that photography was out of the question. Still I hoped Dee would see her moose and I would win our bet. No such luck. By this time we were all but physically shot. The only viable alternative in such cases—at least for us—is to shut up, bury our eyes in the trail ahead and just keep putting one foot in front of the other.

In this manner we covered the remaining two miles to the trailhead. Rather than dwell on my aching knees and sore feet, I envisioned those incredible golden trout with their delicate golden-yellow flanks decorated with brilliant orange ovals and emblazoned below with crimson reminiscent of a vibrant rose. Every fly angler, I thought, should have the opportunity, at least once, to experience golden trout high in the alpine country.

Darkness had enveloped us now, but we were already crossing the last meadow, just a few hundred yards from the truck. I didn't remember the two broad trees that now cast dim moonlit shadows over the far corner of the meadow, but then again I'd been bent on golden trout earlier. A horse trailer, which had been parked there this morning, took shape beyond the two trees at which time I realized those trees must instead be the horses set out to graze. The trail led directly toward the horses.

I stopped so suddenly that Dee almost plowed into me. From 50 feet away, those horses had taken on a slightly different shape. Massive antlers glistening in the moonlight punctuated the most awesome bull moose I'd ever seen. Beside him was a single cow. They watched for a moment and then started toward us as if our presence was as inconsequential as the sage brush they were trampling on their way to the stream opposite us.

As I had not yet said a word, Dee was just then realizing what was ambling toward us. As the potential consequence of our position in line with the bull moose's path became apparent to Dee, I leaned back and whispered, "Now was that $10 for any moose or $10 for each moose?"

Both animals passed too close for comfort as we beat a quiet retreat. After passing by, the moose started into a gallop and the last we heard of them was a loud splashing as they crossed the stream. A coyote trotted off across the meadow and then all was silent, save the incessant crickets, as the moon cast a quiet glow across the Wind River Mountains.

Dee finally remembered to breathe. "That was definitely worth twenty bucks," she said.

Where to Find Golden Trout and Grayling

Oregon tried golden trout in a couple lakes in the Eagle Cap Wilderness, but the program was discontinued long ago and the fish from those initial stocks have long since died out. Washington offers a single grayling lake, which was established through initial plants in 1947. In addition, the state of Washington maintains a hatchery program for golden trout, with some 12-15,000 eggs hatched each year. These fish are distributed in some three dozen lakes throughout the Cascade Mountains (and a few in the Olympics). While listing these lakes would lead directly to my downfall, I will say that you can look up stocking records with the state fisheries department to find out where golden trout live. If you don't have the time or the inclination to dig up the records, try catching a biologist at a weak moment and you may at least find out which drainage to explore for goldens.

Idaho is similar to Washington in that the grayling and golden trout programs are limited in extent. The mountains of central Idaho boast several golden trout lakes, but you need to do your homework to find them. In other words, dig through stocking records. If you catch the right biologist on the right day, you might learn which drainages to explore for golden trout, but you'll be hard pressed to get any lake names. Pretty much the same thing goes for grayling.

The strongest golden trout populations occur in the mountains of Wyoming. For those willing to do a little homework and then a fair amount of legwork, the three wilderness areas encompassing the Wind River Mountains form something of a golden trout/grayling Mecca. These three wilderness areas—the Bridger Wilderness, Popo Agie Wilderness and Fitzpatrick Wilderness—span hundreds of thousands of acres and offer literally hundreds of fishable lakes, many of which contain goldens and grayling. For more details about these areas, see *Alpine Angler: A Fly Fisher's Guide to the Western Wilderness* (Frank Amato Publications, 1995).

Golden trout are native to two streams in California's High Sierra. During the early part of this century, golden trout eggs were traded to other states where hatchery programs

As evidenced by these photos, golden trout vary widely in color but are always beautiful.

were initiated. Wyoming's golden trout program is the most extensive and successful of these. In fact, during its surplus years, Wyoming still trades a few golden trout eggs and fry with other states.

Obviously, finding golden trout or grayling during your alpine-lake trip requires that you do your homework ahead of time. I go about this task rather systematically, first determining which wilderness areas contain populations of goldens or grayling and then do my best to find out which lakes, lake basins or drainages harbor these fish. After deciding where to go, I call the fish and game agency for that state to get whatever information is available. Usually this task will require two or three phone calls—one to the state office to find out which regional office is responsible for overseeing fisheries within the wilderness in question; another call to that regional office and often, in the case of large wilderness areas, yet another call to a second regional office.

When I get through to the regional offices, I ask for the fisheries biologist in charge of high lakes inside the wilderness area. I always call first thing in the morning because the biologists spend lots of time out of the office (in the field or at meetings). Early morning is the best time to catch them at their desks. I ask the biologist about the status of golden trout or grayling populations in the wilderness and I ask if the department publishes any information that might help me find good golden trout/grayling lakes. Examples of such information includes the pamphlet published by the Wyoming Department of Wildlife about the lakes inside the Bridger Wilderness. Similarly, Utah's game department offers a series of small booklets detailing all the lakes in the High Uintas Wilderness in the northeast corner of the state. The Oregon Department of Fish & Wildlife used to publish a series of

pamphlets detailing lakes in each of the national forests (including wilderness areas). These are no longer published, but an enterprising angler might be able to dig up copies somewhere in the ODFW's archives and at least have them photocopied.

Once I've opened up the conversation with questions about the status of the fishery for goldens and grayling and about any available literature, I then go ahead and ask if the biologist has any recommendations about particular lakes or lake basins. Such questions are invariably a crap shoot: sometimes you get lucky and a biologist tells you precisely where to go; other times the biologist either dodges the question or just tells you outright that he really can't tell you about specific lakes.

In the latter case, my follow up question usually goes like this: "Okay, I can certainly understand why you can't tell everybody where golden trout are located, but maybe you could at least tell me what drainage to explore or what side of the range to explore."

More often than not the fisheries people are only too happy to give you general information along those lines and I certainly can't blame them for not telling us exactly where to go. After all, we need to leave something open for discovery. I might add that by making sure the biologist understands that I am willing to work for my fish (e.g. long hikes over rough country) and that I plan to release my goldens and grayling, I have managed to get a few of these folks to open up a little.

In any case, after speaking with the fisheries biologist, you should then call the state fish hatchery responsible for planting fish in the wilderness. You can get the name and number of the hatchery from the state or regional office. Ask to speak with someone familiar with the high lakes stocking

Remote alpine lakes offer solitude and sometimes golden trout or grayling.

program. The hatchery people often seem more willing to divulge information than some biologists. Also ask if stocking records are kept at the hatchery office or at the district office. Find out if you can just show up and peruse the stocking records or if you must make an appointment. These records are public information but that doesn't always mean you will easily gain access to them—a lot depends on how under-staffed the office is at any given time.

After you've gone rounds with the fish and game agency, including the hatchery people, call the U.S. Forest Service office responsible for management of the wilderness area in question. Most large wilderness areas include parts in several ranger districts, so you need to call each district office unless your travels will be restricted to a small portion of the wilderness. In addition to asking about trail conditions, cross-country routes and other such wilderness travel concerns, ask the Forest Service personnel about golden trout and grayling. I've received some awfully good tips from Forest Service folks, themselves fishermen or fisher-women, about which lakes are best and which contain goldens or grayling. A recreation specialist stationed at a ranger station near a central Idaho wilderness area once told me exactly where I could find both goldens and big cutthroat. He had visited the place just a week prior to my conversation with him. Two weeks later I was into foot-long goldens and two-pound cutthroat in a remote glacial cirque lake high in the Idaho mountains.

Finally, don't forget to call local sporting goods stores and fly shops. Visit any major library and you can find phone books for just about every community in America. Or do what I usually do: Call information for the communities nearest your destination and ask for the chamber of commerce or visitor's bureau phone number. Then ask these agencies to give you names and phone numbers of outdoor shops, fly fishing shops and tackle shops.

If you spend the time (and sometimes it will take a lot of phone calls) to ferret out as much information as possible, you will spend a lot more time catching goldens and graylings and a lot less time looking for them.

Naturally, discovery is a thoroughly enjoyable part of the process: You scramble up a 2,000-foot rock slide and find an exquisitely beautiful cirque dotted with turquoise-colored lakes of all sizes and shapes. You spend the next two days fishing each and every lake and catching cutthroat after cut-throat. As lovely as the little cutthroat might be, you press onward up the mountain until you scramble to the top of a ridge and see another series of lakes draining in the opposite direction. Carefully you pick your way down to the first lake, unfurl your line and cast along a rocky shoreline, the lake's white-sand bottom magnified by water the color of a tropical sea. You spot two trout cruising leisurely in your direction, right along the shoreline. By happenstance, your little dry fly is sitting in just the right place. The nearest trout glides silently to the surface, confidently gulping the fly and turning downward again just as you raise the rod tip. A short, lively tussle ensues, after which you beach a trout whose colors take your breath away: a golden trout. The perfect fish for this per-fectly vibrant alpine setting.

Fishing For Golden Trout and Grayling

In some places (especially in Washington and on a few lower elevation lakes in Idaho, Wyoming and Montana) you

A colorful golden trout from Wyoming.

will find golden trout in lakes well below timberline. The focus of this chapter, however, is to introduce you to those goldens and grayling that occupy the true alpine country—at or above timberline and in some of the West's most remote and beautiful country.

In most cases, golden trout and grayling that live at 10, 11, or 12,000 feet don't often have the luxury of feeding in a selective manner. Certainly an evening Chironomid emer-gence can at times cause selective feeding even at 12,000 feet, as can a heavy hatch of *Callibaetis* mayflies ("speckled wing duns"). Far more frequently, however, alpine trout and grayling will eat anything that looks edible.

These fish spend much of their day wandering slowly about the lake or a part of the lake looking for food. Often they hold or wander around the mouth of a tributary stream or near the mouth of the outlet streams. At times they hide under shaded banks and submerged logs or limbs, waiting for food to come to them.

Whichever of these feeding strategies they employ, high-country goldens and grayling generally prove pretty easy to catch so long as anglers avoid spooking them. The exception to this generality occurs in heavily fished waters, but such places are not the focus of this chapter. Instead, we are con-cerned with those lakes that are hard enough to reach that few anglers ply their waters in any given season. In these remote alpine lakes, golden trout and grayling simply must eat everything they can find or face the very real prospect of starving to death. Most alpine lakes are comparatively sterile in relation to lower elevation waters. This is a result of cold water and short growing seasons. After all, many lakes above 10,000 feet remain ice-free for a scant three months each year.

Knowing that these high-altitude fish will be reasonably easy to catch if I can avoid spooking them, I keep my flies and tackle to a minimum. The less tackle I carry, the lighter my backpack will be, so I generally carry a single fly box, one extra leader, one spool each of 5X and 6X tippet material, a floating line on the reel and a sinking line on an extra spool, a pair of leader nippers and a small pair of forceps. In addition, a pair of polarized glasses will prove invaluable. Sometimes I pack along a float tube, fins and waders—depends on how difficult a hike I anticipate. Rarely will you find a lake in which you can't catch plenty of fish from shore, although the float tube offers a distinct advantage at times.

Large golden trout like this one are the trophies sought by serious alpine-country anglers.

If I do lug the float tube along, I choose waders based on the length and difficulty of the hike: 3mm neoprenes keep me warm in the icey alpine waters, but they are heavy and burdensome to pack. Conversely, light-weight nylon waders take up very little space and weight in the backpack, but provide little insulation against the chill of an alpine lake. I frequently opt for the nylon waders, trading warmth for weight (or lack thereof). Then I simply come to shore as soon as I start feeling cold. The new bladder-system float tubes offer a distinct advantage for backpacking anglers. These float tubes feature an inflatable polyethurene bladder that you can blow up by mouth. Uninflated, they can be rolled up into a reasonably small package. My choice is the Premier model tube produced by Caddis Manufacturing of McMinnville, Oregon. The Premier is an open-front-end tube that I can inflate by mouth in about 10 minutes (a little longer when I'm sucking wind at 12,000 feet!).

The majority of the time I leave the float tube behind simply to save on weight in the backpack. An angler afoot can do just fine on most alpine lakes, so long as he or she approaches the water with care. Always fish the shallows first. That means approaching the lake shore very carefully, watching for cruising trout. My basic alpine-lake strategy is simple: Locate the inlets and outlets and fish these places first before moving on to cover other structures like shaded shorelines, steep drop-offs, peninsulas, shoals, log jams and talus slides. Generally speaking, if I don't find trout or grayling hanging out around the major inlets and outlets and I don't see any fish rising after what seems like a reasonable amount of time, I move on to the next lake.

When I do find fish holding at the mouth of a tributary, I like to try a dry fly first. Many alpine lakes feature little if any shoreline cover, save a few big rocks and maybe a handful of stunted trees. In these cases, I drop to all fours and sneak quietly into casting range. Then, from a sitting or kneeling position, I cast into the current of the stream and allow the dry fly (usually a Gulper Special, small Elk Hair Caddis or Renegade) to drift toward the fish waiting a few feet downstream. A little drag on the fly won't bother the fish much at all (sometimes it seems to get them excited), but a sloppy cast will send every one of them scurrying for deep water.

After fishing the inlets in this manner, I look for other likely areas. A few years ago, Dee and I fished a tiny golden trout lake in Wyoming that was loaded with 12- to 16-inch fish. We caught one trout each from both inlets. Then we moved downshore to a deep, narrow bay that lead to the outlet. Kneeling on the shoreline, we cast sinking lines across the bay, allowed the flies (size 10 soft-hackle Zug Bugs) to sink for several seconds and then retrieved with rather fast six-inch strips of line. Every other cast yielded at least a strike and we caught perhaps a dozen or 15 goldens in a half hour's time. Then we walked down the outlet, keeping well back from shore. What we found there, some 20 yards below the lake, was breathtaking: upwards of 80 goldens, in full spawning regalia, paired up on spawning redds. These fish we left alone, but we watched them for a time, the foot-deep pristine water emblazoned by the crimson flanks of these stunningly beautiful trout.

Finding these spawning goldens in the outlet came as no surprise: Golden trout tend to migrate downstream to spawn, so those found in high lakes invariably prefer the outlet stream for spawning activity (assuming appropriate habitat is located there). The fact that goldens migrate downstream to spawn sometimes affects the management of the species. If the trout in a particular lake wind up migrating down an outlet from which they cannot re-enter the lake, stocking efforts are wasted. Sure, the goldens may populate the stream below, but if brook trout or cutthroat are already present, the goldens generally prove to be rather poorly adapted to the competition.

Golden trout and grayling thrive in lakes in some of the most rugged and striking country in the West.

In any case, two weeks later I was back in Wyoming with my fishing buddy Tim Blount. Again we went in search of goldens and again found rather large individuals in a remote glacial cirque. This lake featured a large shoal area just ahead of a rather substantial outlet. A steep drop-off led from this half-acre shoal into the lake proper. The bottom of the three-foot-deep shoal area was entirely visible owing to the superbly clear water, but the drop-off was so abrupt that the tannish bottom of the shallows yielded almost immediately to a deep emerald green.

Early in the morning, trout cruised around on the shallows and we simply cast dry flies out and waited for a trout to swim near. As the sun rose higher, however, the goldens abandoned the shallows in favor of the cover offered by proximity to the deep water. I worked my way around to the other side of the cove while Timmy fished the drop-off from the near side. Each time we could get a fly in the right place—right along the edge of the drop-off—we would generally hook a trout. Too far to either side, however, and hookups were few.

A few days later, Timmy and I found a nice grayling lake where a similar scenario unfolded. We used our float tubes this time. For the first half hour or so, we worked the fishy-looking shallows where we allowed small wet flies to sink some five or six feet before retrieving with slow strips. Without so much as a bump, we decided to rethink our tactics. We switched to sinking lines and moved toward deeper water. Again we found a drop-off where the lake went from six or eight feet to about 15 feet deep. Along the drop-off we began hooking nice grayling of 12 to 15 inches until a thunderstorm ran us off the lake and out of Wyoming.

In the case of those grayling, we were never able to actually see the fish. Instead we just cast sinking lines and retrieved the flies over likely looking areas. Often enough this tactic will prove useful and effective. More exciting, however, are those times when you can cast to visibly cruising trout. Alpine-lake goldens and grayling spend a fair amount of time cruising in shallow water—after all, the shallows hold most of the food because what scant plant life exists in the alpine lakes always grows most profusely where light penetration is greatest. Plant life means insect life. Moreover, the fish stand a greater chance of finding terrestrials (ants, beetles, spiders, bees, etc.) and mayfly spinners near the shoreline.

Large golden trout from Wyoming.

Wyoming's Wind River Range.

Thus alpine-lake anglers have ample opportunity to sight-fish. My favorite tactic for doing this is to cast a fly into the trout's path and then wait for the fish to see the fly. Both dry flies and wet flies work for this technique. In either case you must cast quite a ways ahead of the fish or you risk spooking your quarry with the line and leader splash (even the gentlest splash from a four-weight line can spook trout on a dead-still alpine lake).

If you employ a dry, just allow the fly to sit motionless until the trout cruises by. If the fish doesn't rise, try skating the fly a few inches just as the fish has passed underneath. Sometimes the skated fly will get the fish's attention. With a wet fly, you must lead the trout enough so that the fly can settle to the bottom before the fish gets there. Then, when the fish approaches to within about two feet, begin moving the fly with a series of short, slow strips. Most of the time the fish will dash over and inhale the fly.

Because sight-fishing with a wet fly works best when the fly is allowed to settle all the way to the bottom, you are often better off casting the fly to an area where you have seen several trout or grayling cruising and then simply waiting until another fish wanders near. Any way you decide to handle the situation, sight-fishing to alpine-lake trout and grayling is undoubtedly the most exciting way to take these fish.

Wind can put a damper on sight-fishing strategies since the rippled water hides what lies below. You can no longer see the trout, but then they can't see you as well either. We were sight-fishing to cruising fish in an alpine lake in Montana's Bitterroot Mountains a few years ago, when a typical high-country breeze began blowing across the lake, forming a gentle chop on the surface just off shore. Dee was doing most of the fishing, so I climbed up a little higher on the slope behind her. From my vantage point, I was able to see into the water somewhat, despite the breeze. When I spotted a trout, I would direct Dee on where to cast and we ended up tag-teaming several nice fish that way.

Wind also deposits lots of new food onto a lake's surface, especially if the shoreline is cloaked with a few conifers. Ants are a common item in the diet of alpine-lake fish, so I often dig out a black ant pattern and fish below overhanging trees on windy days. The speckled-wing dun mayflies, after they have molted into the spinner stage, invade the shallow areas of the lake where they deposit their eggs and then die on the water. Wind tends to congregate these spinners along the shore toward which the breeze is blowing, thereby attracting fish to that side of the lake. A Gulper Special, Parachute Adams, or similar fly will generally suffice, although sometimes an actual spinner pattern works better. I carry a few *Callibaetis* Krystal Spinners for these occasions (see dressing at the end of this chapter).

Typically, the *Callibaetis* emergence is even more important than the spinner fall. The nymphs of these mayflies, which are found in every high lake, begin swimming about rather restlessly within the hour or so prior to

Effective wet flies for alpine lakes.

Soft-Hackle Zug Bug

Zug Bug

Hare's Ear Nymph

Pheasant Tail Nymph

Partridge & Orange

Timberline Emerger

Woolly Bugger

emergence. Emergence typically begins during mid- to late afternoon when you will begin to see a few rises here and there before you actually notice many mayflies. Then, quite suddenly, more and more duns appear on the surface, where they sit for several seconds before flying away. The trout start rising all over the place. Then a breeze blows through for a few seconds and the mayflies disappear: I think the rippled water causes all kinds of difficulty for the emerging nymphs, which are trying to break through the surface. A few minutes go by and the breeze dies. Again you start seeing more and more mayfly duns on the surface. This time the breeze holds off for a while and a truly respectable hatch develops. The mayflies seem to hatch in waves, but to one degree or another they emerge for 45 minutes or an hour. Such is the typical alpine *Callibaetis* emergence.

If you are familiar with the precise timing of the mayfly hatch on a particular lake, you can fish a small Pheasant Tail Nymph or *Callibaetis* Nymph prior to the emergence and expect excellent results. When the hatch begins in earnest, a Gulper Special or similar dry fly will usually suffice. Just cast the fly in the vicinity of rising trout and then wait. If you get tired of waiting, skate the fly ever so gently.

The other hatch of major significance to alpine-lake golden trout and grayling is that of the Chironomid (midges). These insects, typically quite small, comprise the most abundant trout food in high lakes. They are most available during the hatches, which can occur any time of day, depending on weather and water temperature. The evening midge emergences are generally the heaviest and most important. While a Chironomid emergence on a fertile reservoir or spring creek can cause ultra-selective feeding on the trout's part, these same hatches at 12,000 feet are much easier to handle most of the time. I generally use two flies: A Griffith's Gnat as a dropper and, some two or three feet below, a Chironomid pupa pattern (dressings given in Chapter 4). I generally employ the cast-wait-skate routine wherein I cast toward rising fish, wait for a minute or more and then slowly retrieve the flies with slow line strips. Often the trout hit one of the flies before I begin the retrieve.

Those two hatches—midges and speckled-wing dun mayflies—comprise the most significant hatches on the golden trout and grayling waters of the Western high country. Most of the lakes have populations of rather large caddisflies; their sparse emergences can drive trout nuts. A few big caddis adults, freshly emerged and trying to take flight by skittering about on the surface, will certainly get golden trout or grayling looking up. So I always carry a few size 8 and 10 olive Jugheads or Bucktail Caddis. These can be greased with floatant and then skated slowly along on the surface. These caddis hatches tend to be sparse and sporadic during the day, but at dusk and thereafter the adults come back to lay their eggs by landing on the water and running across the surface (in some cases by diving under). These egg-laying flights can be rather profuse, with more insects on the water than seems possible judged by the sparseness of the daily emergences.

Other typical stillwater trout foods are found in the alpine lakes: Damsels, scuds, dragonfly nymphs, water beetles and leeches. Rarely have I seen lakes above timberline with enough of any one of these organisms to cause selective feeding. Most of the time, in fact, the golden trout and grayling of

Productive dry flies for alpine lakes.

the alpine country are more than eager to eat lots of different fly patterns. Most important on these waters is the need to be careful and unobtrusive in your approach.

Flies For Golden Trout and Grayling

I've often felt that anglers who hike the brutally rugged routes into some of the more remote alpine lake basins should be rewarded with dumb trout. In fact, I'd like to see some kind of relative dumbness worked out: The longer and harder the hike, the dumber the trout when you get there. Luckily, with alpine-lake golden trout and grayling, this scenario comes close to being true a lot of the time. Living in remote, comparatively infertile waters at high altitude, alpine-lake trout don't often enjoy the luxury of selective feeding. Instead, they must take what they can find when they find it. Thus fly choice for alpine grayling and goldens can be kept rather simple. I use a handful of favorite general-use wet flies and dry flies and switch to hatch-matching flies only on those few occasions when an emergence of Chironomids or speckled-wing dun mayflies causes selective feeding. In addition to those flies listed below, I usually carry Hare's Ear Nymphs, small Woolly Buggers, Flying Ants (black, size 10-14), Gulper Specials (size 14-16), Renegades (size 12-16), Griffith's Gnats (size 14-20) and Elk Hair Caddis (size 10-16).

Soft-hackle Zug Bug

Hook: *Wet fly, 2XL, No. 10-14*
Tail: *Peacock sword*
Body: *Peacock herl*
Rib: *Fine silver or gold oval tinsel*
Collar: *Partridge hackle (standard Zug Bug has throat of brown hackle fibers)*
Wingpad: *Wood duck breast*

Partridge & Orange (Sylvester Nemes)

Hook: *Wet fly, No. 8-14*
Body: *Orange silk*
Collar: *Two turns of natural hare's ear fur*
Hackle: *Two turns of partridge*

Pheasant Tail Nymph

Hook: *Wet fly, 2XL, No. 10-14*
Tail: *Pheasant tail fibers*
Body: *Pheasant tail ribbed with counter of fine wire*
Wingcase and Legs: *Pheasant tail fibers pulled over thorax with tips folded back for legs*
Thorax: *Peacock herl*

Timberline Emerger (Randall Kaufmann)

Hook: *Wet fly, No. 12-14*
Tail: *Brown hackle fibers or partridge fibers*
Body: *Gray-brown dubbing*
Throat: *Brown hackle or partridge*
Wing: *Two grizzly hackle tips*

Callibaetis Krystal Spinner

Hook: *Dry fly, No. 12-18*
Tails: *Micro fibetts or hackle fibers, divided*
Body: *Tan dubbing*
Wings: *About six strands of Krystal Flash, tied spent to both sides*
Hackle: *Dun-grizzly mixed, wound through the wings, clipped below*

Chapter VI

Crappie

A handsome crappie from an eastern Oregon reservoir. This fish took a tiny marabou jig fished on a six-weight fly rod.

It began as one of those spill-your-coffee-on-your-crotch-on-the-way-out-of-the-driveway days and no decent fishing trip ever starts that way. Bad enough that I was already running late. I told Tim 6 a.m., but picked him up at 7:30. I slouched behind the steering wheel, barely saying a word. I've never been much of a morning person and a lapful of coffee wasn't helping.

Six hours later we stopped a few yards from the shoreline of a desolate sage-country reservoir. Studying the reservoir, we picked a section of shoreline that offered a gentle slope, firm bottom and a handful of flooded brushpiles. When in doubt, we always fish cover and those brushpiles looked promising.

Tim hooked a crappie on the first cast and for the next two hours we caught crappie so fast that a fishless cast was virtually out of the question. Just for variety, we drove around to the other end of the reservoir and struck a few more nice crappie, although the gold mine we had found initially soon lured us back to begin anew.

The day disappeared too fast, as they always do when fishing is at its best. The whole affair had been easy—ridiculously easy. And we loved every minute of it. Just as there exists a certain inherent charm to luring a selective trout to a dry fly, so too is their a special pleasure in bagging a hundred crappie in a day.

The next day proved a carbon-copy of the first and our enthusiasm never dampened in the least. Perhaps I will never again enjoy such fabulous crappie fishing as we lucked into that weekend, but rest assured I will certainly keep trying for a repeat—crappie on a fly rod are worth the effort. Indeed, that was the first time I ever had good fishing on a trip that began with a lapful of hot coffee.

The road out was only barely a road. We bounced and bumped along for some 20 miles before hitting pavement. A short while later we arrived at a small desert town.

In a cloud of chalky dust, we skidded to a stop in front of the town's only open establishment—a tavern of apparent ill-repute half-filled with patrons of obvious ill-repute whom I only hoped didn't represent the citizenry at large.

Coffee was on and judging by its texture, it had been on for the better part of the weekend. The bartender filled my cup and then nuked the whole works in a pre-ice-age microwave.

That accomplished, we groped our way through the haze of cigarette smoke, found the door, and, in turn, the truck (with all of its hubcaps still intact). With hundreds of crappie still dancing in our heads, I jammed the Ford into gear and immediately doused my lap with coffee again.

Where To Find Northwest Crappie

One of the crappie's endearing features is its relative abundance: You can find them within easy reach of virtually any town in the Northwest. Some of the traditional hotspots include the Seep Lakes of eastern Washington and Brownlee Reservoir on the Oregon/Idaho border. But crappie live and thrive all over the Northwest, from the sloughs on the Willamette and Columbia to some of the high-desert reservoirs of eastern Oregon and southern Idaho.

If I could rank my favorite crappie haunt, Brownlee Reservoir would probably be number one, but a lot of other people feel that way as well, so Brownlee is usually rather crowded. If you want solitude, seek out the lesser-known waters. A call to the fish and game in any of the Northwest states will put you in touch with good crappie prospects (ask to speak with the warmwater specialist in the respective departments).

Timing Your Crappie Trip

Without doubt the easiest time to find crappie is during their spring spawning period when the fish invade shallow water en masse. East of the Cascades, the spawning period occurs with the first hot-weather spell, usually sometime during May. In western Oregon and western Washington, the crappie spawn may begin as early as March or as late as May, depending on the weather.

Water temperature generally determines the precise timing of the spawn. Crappie begin moving into the shallows as water temperatures warm to the mid-50s. When the water temperature reaches the high 50s to mid-60s, most spawning activity will begin. In off-color reservoirs (which are common throughout the Northwest), crappie spawn in one to five feet of water. In clear water, they seem to prefer deeper spawning beds, often eight or 15 feet below the surface.

Naturally, the crappie spawn is never one big unified affair. Instead, it is drawn out over a week or more as different parts of the lake warm faster than others. During the actual spawning period, which might last a day or several days, crappie don't show much interest in feeding. However, since individual fish don't all spawn at once, you can always catch fish once you locate spawning habitat.

Prior to the actual spawn, crappie gather in "staging areas" outside the actual spawning grounds. This pre-spawn period can produce the best crappie fishing of the year, with fish remaining in these areas for several weeks until the water temperatures warm enough to lure them onto the spawning grounds. During the weeks leading up to the spawn, search for concentrations of fish off long points, near tributary streams, at the mouth of small bays and coves and just off shelves and steep slopes near shallow benches and shorelines. If you fish the reservoirs of southern Idaho and eastern Oregon (e.g. Brownlee Reservoir, Owyhee Reservoir), pay special attention to gently sloping shorelines featuring shale bottoms. These places usually serve as spawning grounds for crappie.

If these areas include some kind of structure (pilings, stumps, logs, flooded snags and the like) so much the better. Crappie are structure-oriented fish, although structure to crappie in a barren reservoir might mean little more than a sudden drop-off or old stream channel. Still, locating structural elements that attract crappie will help substantially in finding fish. After the spawn, the females begin to leave the shallows, leaving the male fish to guard and tend the nest. After the eggs hatch (a week or so) the males will usually guard the fry until they disperse from the nest.

DeAnn Shewey with a big grin and a big Northwest crappie.

What this amounts to—the pre-spawn period and the spawning season itself—is several weeks of excellent opportunity to find crappie in depths of three to 15 feet of water.

After the males have left the nest, they too move into slightly deeper water, often concentrating around structures such as weed beds, flooded brush or timber and drop-offs or channels. Meanwhile, water temperatures begin to climb toward summer peaks.

During summer, concentrate your efforts near cover in deeper water. Look for drop-offs and flooded timber or find creek channels, ledges or stumps in 10 to 20 feet of water. Naturally, a depth finder is a great help in locating crappie cover and the fish themselves (especially those that are suspended above or beside cover), but an observant eye can locate likely areas: Study shoreline features to gain an understanding of what lies below the surface. Look for tributary streams that might offer channels; steep cliffs, rock slides or road embankments that indicate drop-offs and rock piles; stumps on the shore that might indicate additional stumps on the reservoir bottom. If you can locate a topographical map of the reservoir you're fishing, you can find old channels, drop-offs and other likely crappie haunts.

Use the countdown method with a sinking line to fish different depths until you hit fish. Float tube trolling is an effective

Spring spawning season is the ideal time for fly rod crappie because the fish are concentrated in the shallows. Here DeAnn Shewey fishes a shale-bed on Brownlee Reservoir—the shale bottom areas seem to be preferred by the crappie during the spawning season.

method for locating crappie as well, especially those fish suspended over rock piles, ledges or weeds. Use a fast-sinking line and allow the line to sink to the bottom before you start trolling. Then kick slowly so the line remains at an effective depth while employing a few strips and controlled line releases to add erratic movement to the fly.

Without question the easiest time to find crappie is during the pre-spawn and spawning season. However, anglers who find and fish appropriate cover later in the summer can experience fishing every bit as fast and furious as that of the spawning period.

Autumn fishing can be difficult if water temperatures change quickly and drastically (as they sometimes do on the desert reservoirs of eastern Washington, eastern Oregon and southern Idaho), but given a gradual change in water temperatures, you can still find decent crappie fishing if you concentrate on good cover. During both late fall and winter, crappie tend to hold near the bottom, where they still feed actively. Thus mid-winter fishing can be productive once you locate a school of fish. Look for channels, ridges or humps in 10 to 30 feet of water.

Winter and early spring, in fact, usually comprise a stable time of year for crappie. They remain in the same areas for weeks or months on end, feeding actively. If you find a concentration of fish during the winter, you can likely catch crappie in that spot just about any time you are willing to brave the weather. They may hold at different depths, but will typically remain in the same general vicinity.

Incidentally, if you venture afield (for whatever purpose) during winter, take time to study crappie reservoirs that have been drawn down for the winter months. Locate

likely structure (stumps, channels, brush piles, rock piles, etc.) that will again be flooded come summer: You will probably find crappie at these places later in the year. Likewise, recent years have seen substantial drawdowns on Snake River and Columbia River reservoirs during the late spring: These spring drawdowns are an attempt to help flush salmon and steelhead smolt out of the rivers and into the ocean.

If you take the time to study the bottom features of a particular reservoir during low-water periods, you can easily locate and chart structure that will hold crappie when the reservoirs fill later in the year. During the spring of 1994, for example, Brownlee Reservoir dropped two feet during one of our weekend trips. We located numerous anchored brushpiles (installed by the Fish and Game Department) that would hold crappie as soon as the reservoir filled again.

Bear in mind that crappie tend to use the same structures over and over: If you find fish there once, you'll likely find them again. Therefore, if you get serious about crappie fishing, jot down notes to help you remember where you find fish. If possible, mark such locations on a map.

Tactics For Crappie

Crappie feed on a variety of organisms, with minnows and aquatic insects being most significant. Large crappie tend to feed on minnows and fry more than small crappie, a fact which can be of paramount importance in waters where crappie grow to impressive sizes: These fish can be selective and at times will ignore small nymphs and jigs while jumping all over minnow patterns like Marabou Muddlers, Zonkers or Woolly Buggers.

If you fish during the pre-spawn and spawning periods, you won't likely run into many selective crappie. During this time, just about any fly or mini-jig will catch fish if presented at the crappie's level. Mini-jigs (from 1/32 ounce to 1/80 ounce) can be very effective when the crappie are in the shallows. These small marabou jigs are easy to cast with a fly rod. As an added bonus, they are a lot less expensive than most flies. Black is always good and I've done well with chartreuse and white jigs (and flies) also. If casting a tiny jig offends your sense of fly fishing etiquette, then try a Woolly Bugger, Woolly Worm, or Girdle Bug.

I prefer a fairly slow retrieve simply because the fish often take the fly or jig during the pause between line strips. A slow retrieve, with an exaggerated pause, allows them every opportunity to do this.

After the spawn, when crappie return to deeper water, fly anglers should be prepared to use a variety of methods. Most important, however, is locating fish. I use any of several attractor patterns on a sinking line or sink-tip line and cast to likely looking cover. With each successive cast I fish shallower (or deeper, depending on whether you want to start fishing deep or start shallow). If I hit a crappie, I continue fishing at that level.

Sometimes, even though you have located a school, the crappie may hit the fly infrequently. When this happens, and you are reasonably certain you are fishing at the appropriate depth, try changing speeds, either switching to an ultra-slow, erratic retrieve or employing a quick retrieve. If changing your retrieve pattern fails to entice more fish, try a different fly. I often start with a mini-jig or small Woolly Bugger. If these fail, I switch to a small nymph (such as a Soft-hackle Hare's Ear or small Girdle

Bug) or to a minnow imitation (Marabou Muddler or Zonker).

One of my favorite tricks for crappie (not to mention smallmouth bass and bluegill) is to fish a small nymph (size 10 or 12) below a larger streamer (e.g. a size 6 white Marabou Muddler). The larger fly gets their attention, but often they eat the small fly instead.

During summer and early fall, crappie may even feed at the surface during insect hatches, so a selection of basic dry flies (Adams', Parachute Adams', Renegades, Griffith's Gnats) will come in handy.

Tim Blount introduced me to a technique that has become standard operating procedure anytime we are into crappie: Before lifting the fly from the water for your next cast, hold the rod still so the fly or jig hangs motionless a foot or so beneath the surface. Even if the crappie refuse to strike during your retrieve, they often follow the lure until it stops, at which time they devour the fly. Thus our typical pattern features a patient, slow retrieve with frequent pauses followed at the end with a fly held motionless near the surface, the angler's arm and rod reaching out over the water to keep direct contact with the fly.

In any case, once you find a school of crappie, you can generally figure out a way to catch them. So invest your energy in locating and fishing prime areas, but don't spend too much time in one place: Fish an area thoroughly enough to satisfy yourself that no fish are present (10 or 15 minutes) and then move on. Sooner or later you will find the fish. Once you locate a school, fish until things slow down and then move somewhere else. Return to the original spot an hour or two later, after the crappie have regrouped.

Prior to and during the late-spring spawning period, crappie can be caught in shallow water. Later, the fish will move to deeper areas for the balance of the year.

Tim Blount with a nice white crappie from
Brownlee Reservoir.

Incidentally, since crappie are structure-oriented, don't
hesitate to cast around bridge pilings, marina docks and other
such man-made features. These places sometimes produce
exceptional catches.

During the peak of summer, when light intensity is at its
height, crappie seem to feed most heavily around dusk and
dawn, including well after dark. Sometimes a reservoir, pond
or slough that seemed devoid of crappie during the day will
come alive at dusk.

At dusk on many crappie waters, minnows and other bait-
fish (not to mention emerging aquatic insects) concentrate
near the surface in shallow water. This activity lends itself
perfectly to a dry line and a small streamer pattern fished just
inches below the surface.

Night-fishing for crappie, meanwhile, is perhaps the
most unappreciated method in the Northwest. If you want
total solitude in your fishing and a chance at some exceptional shallow-water crappie fishing, dig out a Coleman
lantern and go to work. The lantern, when allowed to hang
over the water from a tree limb, mooring, piling, or long
pole, will attract plankton and in turn minnows. These food
organisms then attract crappie. (Some mail-order houses
and a few sporting goods stores sell "crappie lights" that
float.)

Similarly, you can expect to find night-feeding crappie
around man-made light sources where appropriate structure is
located. Such places might include bridge lights, dock lights,
or marina lights. In short, if you live near crappie water,
consider trying your luck at night. If you travel to one of the
Northwest's numerous crappie reservoirs, try fishing for a
couple hours after dark, preferably with the aid of artificial
light. Sometimes the action can be surprisingly furious.

Marabou Muddler

Hook: *Streamer, No. 6-10*
Body: *Gold diamond braid*
Wing: *Marabou: white, black or yellow; a few strands of
    Krystal Flash; topped with peacock sword*
Collar: *Deer hair*
Head: *Deer hair, spun and clipped*

Woolly Bugger

Hook: *Streamer, No. 4-8*
Tail: *Marabou and a few strands of Krystal Flash*
Body: *Chenille*
Hackle: *Saddle hackle or rubber legs*
Rib: *Fine gold to bind down hackle*
Eyes: *Lead eyes (optional)*
Colors: *Black, olive, brown, green, white*

Zonker (Dan Byford)

Hook: *Streamer, No. 4-6-8*
Body: *Pearlescent or gold Mylar tubing*
Wing: *Rabbit strip: white, black, yellow or chartreuse*

Soft-hackle Zug Bug

Hook: *Nymph or wet fly, No. 8-10*
Tail: *Peacock sword*
Body: *Peacock herl*
Rib: *Fine gold or silver oval*
Collar: *Two turns of partridge hackle*

Soft hackle Hare's Ear Nymph

Hook: *Nymph or wet fly, No. 8-12*
Tail: *Partridge fibers*
Body: *Natural hare's mask fur*
Rib: *Fine gold oval*
Thorax: *Natural dark hare's mask fur*
Wingcase: *Olive Krystal Flash or dark turkey quill segment*
Collar: *Two turns of partridge hackle*

Tuck's Bug (Dave Tucker)

Hook: *3XL streamer, No. 6-10*
Tail: *Soft white hackle fibers*
Body: *Chartreuse chenille*
Throat: *Red hackle fibers (optional)*

Chapter VII

Winter Steelhead

Ray Slusser, a guide from Oregon, took this beautiful winter steelhead from the Rogue River. Ray Slusser photo

As a child, growing up in the semi-wilds of southeast Idaho, I'd never heard of winter steelhead or any other kind of steelhead. I was too busy to worry about such things, preferring to spend most of my idle time devising ways to maim and torment myself. This was necessary, as doing so prevented me from wasting valuable time trying to kill myself.

I would have been happy to use my siblings in my various ingenious experiments, but my older sister was a lot tougher than me and my younger brother was a lot smarter than me. Come to think of it, my sister was both tougher and smarter than me and I'm not real certain that my brother started out smarter: I think maybe I helped educate him to the point that he just wasn't any fun anymore.

Up until about the age of eight, he was a pretty good subject. I used to challenge him to a punching contest: "Hey Mike, let's see who can punch the softest—you go first..." He'd deliver the most delicate of blows to my left shoulder. Then I'd clobber him with the hardest right cross I could muster. "You win again, Mike."

Naturally, he smartened up right quick after a few such episodes. About the tenth time I tried to sucker him in for that routine, his eyes lit up when I told him he could go first. You can pretty much figure the rest out. After that he wanted no part of my attempts to smoke out a crusty old badger from a nearby hillside; nor did he harbor much desire to help with my early experiments in pyrotechnics, which involved smoke-

less powder (or sort-of smokeless powder), .22 cartridges and shotgun shell primers. I still have all my fingers, but suffice it to say my background as a designer of fireworks was short-lived, as was my perfect hearing.

In any case, I was left with little choice but to serve as the guinea pig in my own experiments.

Have you ever wondered why downhill ice-skating is not an Olympic event? Rest assured I can explain it to you. Likewise I can tell you in no uncertain terms that golfball-sized spit wads don't go over well when splattered all over the chalkboard in the fifth grade. Nor does aiding the substitute teacher in unclogging a big bottle of Elmer's Glue by stomping on it. (For that matter, having spent a fair percentage of my elementary-school sentence incarcerated in the vice-principal's office, I can assure you that laughing at the VP's attempts to inflict physical reprimand will win no points either.)

Despite my voluminous attempts at getting suspended from grade school, my real forte' lay in devising ways to damage myself as a budding young outdoorsman. Some of my most impressive feats involved Opening Days:

Opening Day, age 9: I climb up a split-rail fence near the creek, jump enthusiastically off the far side and promptly drive a three-inch rusted nail through my foot. Tetanus shots go over well on Opening Day.

Opening Day, age 10: I trespass carefully through the Old Grouch's apple orchard, intent on fishing waters rarely fished

The North Umpqua on a winter day. Many Northwest rivers, the North Umpqua included, host runs of both summer and winter steelhead, assuring that there are fish in the river every month of the year.

on account of the Old Grouch's temper and a .22 single-shot. I promptly encounter a swarm of hornets that prove devoid of any sense of humor and sprint through the nearest exit from the orchard, consequently running into the Old Grouch's two Dobermans (these also lacking any sense of humor) and flying by the Old Grouch himself so fast that I barely notice the satisfied chuckles emanating from the Old Grouch. Upon later relating the tale to the neighborhood kids I am roundly disbelieved on account of nobody ever having seen or heard of the Old Grouch so much as crackling a smile let alone chuckling outright.

Opening Day, age 11: Stalking carefully downstream through ankle-deep water on my way to a favorite pool, I climb the split rail fence spanning the creek as I have done many times before. The single strand of wire—electric-fence wire—running along the top of the fence supported by little insulating devices causes no concern as I have never known the wire to run hot. But this is Opening Day. With soaking wet feet I straddle the fence as usual with no regard to the wire only to wake up a few seconds later lying on my back in the middle of the creek and feeling as if a mule had just kicked me in the chest.

It should be rather apparent why I hold little regard these days for Opening Day. In fact, deciding Opening Day was against my religion has pretty much unburdened a lot of my fishing excursions, providing me with streams and lakes devoid of other anglers. That, of course, is another story altogether.

In any case, those Opening Days of my youth exemplify many of my early attempts to massacre myself. Not that those particular episodes were isolated: I made a regular habit of studying the relative sense of humor amongst bee and hornet swarms and I can assure you that I never did find a single swarm whose members displayed even the slightest grasp of light-hearted gaiety. Likewise, I used to be considered something of a

hero amongst the neighborhood kids when it came to showing off scars from rusty nails. And my affinity for electric fences led to my later attempts at making a human lightning rod of myself.

By the sixth grade I had expanded the scope of my efforts to include combination experiments. I mixed my interest in venomous critters like rattlers and scorpions with my mastery of pyrotechnics; trespassing got too easy so I added range bulls and a biker gang to the mix of things to be avoided while sneaking through places I wasn't welcome.

But my life soon took what at the time seemed like an unfortunate turn: We moved to Oregon. Suddenly thrust into town life in western Oregon, my opportunities for self-mutilation in the outdoors seemed rather bleak.

Then I discovered winter steelhead.

Not that I believed in the actual existence of these critters called steelhead. After all, the first two years I fished for them, I never saw a fish. But the opportunity to be outdoors and try to kill myself was well worth the frustration of fishing for a creature whose existence I sometimes question to this day.

It all started with a couple of bad winters in Oregon—the kind reminiscent of those ice-your-guides-up days of early spring back in eastern Idaho. One of those winters coincided with my junior year in high school, which in turn coincided with my obtaining a driver's license, which in retrospect seemed a lot like letting the proverbial fox into the hen house.

It was December of that year and I was taking a leave of absence from classes. I was knee-deep in the Salmon River north of Lincoln City while a light snow duked it out with a very cold rain, each trying in turn to exert their dominance. As if not to be outdone, a chilling wind began blowing upriver. My guides froze every few casts, so I had to keep dipping the rod in the river to thaw them. The whole experience, as I recall, ranked right up there with slamming your hand in a car door, which, come to think of it, might not have been so bad since I couldn't feel my fingers anyway.

That's when it happened. I delivered about as pretty a cast as I was capable of, considering the circumstances. The fly, a big, orange Teeny Nymph, landed with a soft splat and sunk into a promising looking current seam just a few yards away. The line drifted downriver, pacing the progress of the fly. Just as the line tightened at the end of the drift, the water erupted in front of me. Unfortunately, my fly and the eruption had nothing to do with one another. Instead, a monstrous old Chinook had breached mere feet in front of me, scaring the hell out of me to the point that I lost my footing in the already fast current and did a graceful little butt-plant in the absurdly cold water.

I managed to regain my footing ever so briefly before again taking a seat in the river. It was then that I realized my old tennis shoes probably weren't the best wading boots on the market. Eventually I made it back to the car, where I swore off winter steelheading forever—a vow which lasted for about two weeks as I recall. Luckily, subsequent years found me experimenting with more sane ways of suffering in the winter—like duck hunting and night-fishing for rockfish.

Thus my winter steelheading days dwindled rather drastically in number to the point that, these days, I feel pretty lucky if I can add one or two attempted drownings to my record each winter while pursuing steelhead. In fact, I guess that makes for a good way to define success for those who persist in fly fishing for winter steelhead: If your number of fish hooked each winter outnumbers your attempted drownings, I'd say you're way ahead of me.

That is unless you count style points—after all, I can pull off a near-drowning with the best of them.

Strategies For Winter Steelhead

Winter steelhead, by way of definition, are those races of fish that enter the streams between late fall and early spring. Certainly some rivers host late fall runs of summer steelhead; other waters feature what we might call "spring" steelhead. The true winter steelhead—most of which ascend the rivers between December and early March—is a beast living by a slightly different conception of time than the summer fish.

Summer steelhead tend to go about their migration in a rather leisurely manner. After all, they have all summer and all fall before spawning time rolls around during winter. A winter steelhead, conversely, is a fish on a mission—get up to the spawning grounds and get right to the business of reproducing. This is one of the important distinctions between summer steelhead and winter steelhead: The amount of time each spends in fresh water prior to spawning tends to be quite different.

Indeed, winter races and summer races of steelhead tend to go about their respective migrations with slightly differing agendas. The winter fish enter the river systems sexually mature and ready to spawn while the summer steelhead must mature sexually during their time spent in the river.

More important than the precise differences between races of steelhead, however, is the need for fly anglers to adapt their tactics to the cold, high flows of winter. When fishing for winter steelhead fly anglers must usually depart from the classic dry-line, wet-fly swing that draws summer fish to the surface.

Instead, winter steelhead are better approached with a fly fished closer to their level. This does not rule out the wet fly

swing, but rather changes the level at which the fly is allowed to swing across-stream in front of the fish. Much like the dry-line wet-fly swing employed during the summer, the deep wet-fly swing, employing a sink-tip or sinking line, is easy to master and is a more enjoyable and exciting method of taking steelhead than is any variety of dead-drift presentation.

Naturally, winter steelhead anglers must learn to identify good "fly water" on a winter steelhead river. The term "fly water" refers to those places on any given stream where fly-fishing tactics are reasonably easy to employ. Conversely, some water types—especially deep pools and deep, heavy runs—are inherently difficult on fly-rod tactics. So look for water ranging from three to six feet deep, perhaps a little deeper in pools; fish tailouts and the shallower pools, quiet runs and the heads and throats of moderate-speed riffles with adequate depth. Pay special attention to current seams and structure in any of these places. Structure might include gravel bars extending at angles into the river, boulders that break up heavy flows, or ledgerock with rifts and shelves.

Those places that combine depths from three to six feet, perhaps a little more or a little less, and appropriate holding areas, including the aforementioned currents seams and structural elements, comprise what we call fly water. Certainly you can devise tactics for fishing the deepest and the heaviest water, but why torture yourself unless absolutely necessary? Stick to the fly water on any given stream and you will likely find winter steelhead tactics much easier to employ. Besides, the usual crowd of bait and lure anglers that flock to the big pools tend to ignore much of the classic fly water—tailouts, narrow runs and chutes, the top or "head" of the pools and other such places. So let them have the hardware water and you take the fly water.

Winter steelhead streams can change quickly during periods of heavy rain or snowmelt. Rising water, while it might put some fish off the bite, often prompts others to become more active, at least until the water gathers too much speed and color. Those fish which may have spent several hours or days in a rather dour mood, are sometimes awakened by changing water flows, often spurring them to leave deep holding lies and migrate into shallower water on their way upriver.

Unfortunately, however, the same increasing flows that alter a steelhead's mood for better or worse also tend to make

The new-generation sink-tip fly lines allow anglers a wide array of choice. The Jim Teeny fly lines and the STST lines by McKenzie Tackle Company are designed to sink quickly and cast effortlessly.

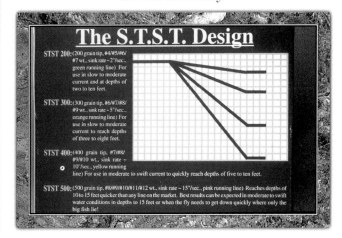

The same showy flies preferred by many anglers for summer steelhead will prove equally effective on winter fish. One need not resort to "string leeches" and lead-head flies when the winter months roll around. Shewey's Golden Eagle.

The Deep Wet-fly Swing

At the heart of any wet-fly swing are two main components: choosing the appropriate kind of fly line to fish at a particular depth and then controlling the speed at which the fly swings across the current.

For fishing a deep swing on small streams, I usually opt for a sink-tip line. Sink tips come in several styles. For deep pools and heavy riffles, the high-density sink-tips marketed by Jim Teeny and by McKenzie Fly Tackle Company of Eugene, Oregon, are perfect. These lines feature high-density tips (24-25 feet long) factory spliced to thin-diameter floating line. The floating section is easy to mend and control on the river's surface while the high-density tip sinks quickly and stays deep during the swing. These lines come in densities ranging from less than 200 grains to about 500 grains. The super-heavy lines (500 grain sink-tips) are burdensome if not suicidal to cast and are rarely needed for winter steelhead fishing. More appropriate for most winter steelhead fishing are the 200- and 300-grain sink-tips, which cast reasonably well on seven-, eight- and nine-weight rods.

On large rivers, I switch to a sinking shooting taper ("shooting head"). My favorite line is a section of high-density (300 or 400 grain) sinking fly line. These are available from the major line companies or you can make your own by cutting the first 20 to 30 feet from a sinking line or sink-tip line. For running line behind this sinking head, I use 25-pound test Amnesia (a brand of monofilament). Amnesia resists kinking and coiling better than most monofilaments and thus rarely forms troublesome knots.

The basic idea with this rigging is to cast across and somewhat downstream and then immediately mend upstream to straighten the line and leader and to place most of the running line upstream from the shooting taper. By setting up the drift in this manner, you gain contact with the fly almost as soon as the cast hits the water, and you are easily able to control the speed of the swing by suspending running line away from the water. (A 10-foot rod will aid in this latter tactic.)

During periods of low, clear water or when fishing shallow runs and pools, I prefer a standard high-density, 10-foot sink-tip line (or sink-tip shooting taper) or a 20- to 30-foot-long sinking shooting taper. These lines, used in the appropriate types of water, will keep the fly deep yet still prevent the fly from snagging repeatedly on streambed rocks. They also cast more easily than the high-density 25-foot sink-tips.

No matter what kind of fly line you employ, keep the leader reasonably short, say three to six feet total, including the 0X or 1X tippet section. Some anglers incorporate a short section of small-diameter lead-core line in the butt-section of the leader to aid in keeping the fly deep. I've tried this technique with favorable results so long as I keep the lead-core section quite short. More than a foot or so in length, and this assemblage causes casting problems. Most of the time, however, the appropriate choice in fly lines coupled with effective control of the fly's swing will enable you to keep the fly at the steelhead's level.

Other than the sinking or sink-tip lines and shortened leaders, the deep swing is identical to the standard dry-line wet-fly swing that we use for summer steelhead (see Chapter 2 of *Northwest Fly Fishing: Trout & Beyond*). The wet-fly swing begins with a down-and-across cast followed immediately by an upstream mend intended to both straighten the leader and provide enough drag-free drift to sink the fly. At the completion of this cast and mend, the fly is allowed to drift until the line

fly fishing more difficult. Flows become heavier, water colors up and the drift of your fly, which must now pass even closer to a fish if you are to have a chance, becomes even more difficult to control. It is under such conditions that a winter steelhead angler hones his or her craft: Nothing teaches you to better control the swing of your fly than being forced to do so in swollen, off-color winter rivers.

When the high flows begin to subside after a storm has moved through, fly anglers can expect their most productive moments of winter. Depending on the particular river, storm run-off or snowmelt run-off from an unusually warm day may begin to clear up within hours or within days. Either way, fly anglers who are on the river when the water drops and clears are fishing the best possible conditions, especially when such conditions are accompanied by reasonably warm weather that warms the water temperature a few degrees.

Spend enough time on your favorite winter steelhead river and you will eventually encounter one of those rare days when the water drops to near-summer levels, when the water temperature increases several degrees and when you can take steelhead on floating line presentations. More often, you will be content to find conditions where falling water allows you access to good fly water where a sink-tip line swings the fly close enough to the steelhead to elicit a violent take.

begins to drag in the current. Then the fly is simply allowed to swing across the current in a long arc under tension from the taut line. The whole operation is really quite simple and can be summarized by the thought that this is one of the few times in stream fishing when we purposely allow the fly to drag.

Different water types dictate slight alterations in the wet-fly swing. In some cases you might mend downstream as the fly swings; other times you mend upstream and still other times you won't need to mend at all after that initial mend is made. The main focus of your mending should be to slow the swing of the fly. In addition to mending line to control the fly's swing, you can also use a controlled line release: As the swinging fly gains momentum, allow fly line to slip slowly through your fingers. To set up this technique, you will need to hold a loop of about six feet of fly line or running line in your free hand. Then, if the fly begins swinging too quickly across-stream, you can allow this loop of line to slide—slowly and deliberately—through the guides.

Dead-Drift Presentations

Dead-drift techniques take winter steelhead as well, but are not as easily mastered as the wet-fly swing. The most significant handicap to dead-drift presentations is that the angler will not always be in direct contact with the fly. Lose contact with the fly and you risk missing takes altogether.

Still, dead-drift techniques can be very effective, especially when steelhead seem disinclined to move off the bottom to chase a swinging fly. If you opt for a dead-drift strategy, you can employ a sinking or sink-tip line like those described above or you can use a floating line coupled with a heavy fly. On those rare occasions when I have felt compelled to indulge in the dead-drift methods, I have generally found the latter set-up—a floating line, long leader and heavy fly—

to be more "controllable" and more effective in all but the heaviest and deepest water.

Naturally, if you fish a dead-drift presentation with any hope of success, you must make sure the fly gets to the bottom. Thus you will cast up and across and immediately mend the line in a manner that will allow the fly to drift unimpeded by drag. Often this means a series of upstream mends, but in certain currents, some combination of upstream mends and downstream mends will be most useful. One highly effective mending technique is what we call the "roll mend" or "stack mend."

The stack mend, which works only with full fly lines and not with shooting tapers, is nothing more than a miniature roll cast delivered after the line is on the water. Make your initial cast up and across, but stop the rod tip rather high. Immediately draw the rod tip into position for a quick roll cast. Then, using the same form needed for a standard roll cast, execute a somewhat underpowered roll, allowing a hoop of line to travel out toward the sink-tip section of your line (if indeed you are using a sink-tip line of some sort). This roll mend allows you to create the slack line needed to sink the flies to the bottom and to extend the drag-free drift. You can deliver this roll mend to either the upstream or downstream side of the line, depending on the demands of particular currents.

Naturally, the dead-drift presentation can be combined with the wet-fly swing simply by allowing the drifting fly to swing across the stream at the end of the drift. Sometimes this combination of both techniques offers the best opportunity to cover a particular run efficiently. Combined, the dead-drift presentation and the wet-fly swing are akin to the "greased-line" method of dry-line steelheading, the only real difference being that, for winter fish, we often employ a sinking or sink-tip line.

Using a 10-foot, high-density sink-tip line, Joe Howell swings a fly through this tailout.

Flies For Winter Steelhead

As with summer steelhead fishing, fly choice for winter steelheading is a thoroughly personal matter. In trout fishing, we often have opportunity to compare relative effectiveness among patterns. Imagine a hatch of mayflies on a spring creek: Trout are feeding selectively, so you choose an imitation for the mayfly in question. After numerous presentations, it becomes rather apparent that a particular trout wants nothing to do with your fly. You choose another pattern—one that imitates the same mayfly, but a different pattern than your initial choice. You hook the trout and go on to hook several more. You can assume with some basis in reason that the choice in patterns was the critical ingredient.

In steelhead fishing, however, we rarely have opportunity to test a fish's comparative response to different patterns. Thus we must choose a fly based on our level of confidence in different patterns or based on the knowledge that getting a fly in front of a steelhead's face is more important than worrying over particular patterns. Alec Jackson used the term "reasonable" to describe fly choice: Just choose a fly that is reasonable and then fish that fly with diligence and confidence. A reasonable fly for an off-color, swollen winter stream might differ considerably from a reasonable fly for that same stream during a low-water period.

In other words, choose a fly that is appropriately matched to the prevailing conditions: Heavy, off-color water might be better suited to larger flies than to small, sparse patterns that we might use in a low, clear stream. I have always been partial to three shades: orange, purple and black. Many of my flies combine these colors and virtually all of my patterns incorporate one or more of these shades. Beyond that, I match sizes to conditions. I like big flies as large as 4/0 in cold and/or off-color water. Rarely, in fact, will I fish steelhead flies smaller than a size 4. I've worked out a series of patterns and sizes that work for me and I leave it at that. Then I fish and fish hard, not worrying about pattern choice.

Granted, a newcomer to steelhead fishing might be overwhelmed by the endless array of steelhead flies. If such is the case, then simply ask a few questions. If you are headed to a particular river, ask those who fish that river about their favorite flies. Or choose two or three flies from the list below and fish them with confidence. Indeed, virtually all of the countless steelhead flies in print today will catch fish somewhere at some time. I further temper my fly choice with my opinion that a steelhead is a majestic enough game fish to deserve nice flies. I won't fish lead-head leeches, string leeches, egg flies, nymphs and other such critters for steelhead simply because I believe a steelhead deserves better. That attitude has involved me in a few arguments over the years, but I simply fish the way I enjoy fishing. Listed below are some of my favorite flies for winter steelhead. This list of patterns represents a mere sampling of what is out there, but these are some of the flies that I like to fish.

Spawning Purple

Hook: *No. 3/0-2*
Tag: *Silver tinsel*
Body: *Flame orange floss*
Wing: *Five spikes of purple marabou, beginning at mid-shank*
Hackle: *Large, purple neck hackle after fourth spike of marabou*
Eyes: *Jungle cock, large*
Collar: *(after eyes are secured) large orange-dyed guinea*

Spawning Purple Hairwing
(originated by Dave McNeese)

Hook: *4/0-2*
Tail: *Orange polar bear or similar and a few strands of Krystal Flash*
Body: *Dubbed seal or Angora goat, hot orange*
Wing: *Three separate wings of purple polar bear or similar, beginning just ahead of mid-shank*
Collar: *A few turns of purple hackle then two turns of natural guinea*

Midnight Canyon

Hook: *No. 4/0-2*
Body: *Rear half silver tinsel, front half black seal or Angora dubbing*
Hackle: *Two black Spey hackles or mix one orange and two black Spey hackles (marabou works best on large sizes— look for plumes with fine stems and minimal fuzz; for small sizes, dyed pheasant rump or similar works fine). Hackles are wound through the body in the Spey style*
Collar: *Gadwall flank*
Wing: *Black goose shoulder sections with one or two strips of orange married through the center of each*
Cheeks: *Jungle cock (optional)*

Orange Angel Spey

Hook: *No. 2/0-4*
Body: *1/2 orange silk, 1/2 orange Angora or seal*
Ribs: *1. medium or wide gold flat trailed by fine gold oval 2. fine or X-fine gold oval as counter*
Hackle: *Hot orange marabou blood plume palmered through front half of body and bound down with countering rib (tips of marabou plume are dipped in black dye)*
Collar: *Dyed-orange mallard flank*
Wing: *White goose shoulder segments, tied tent-style*

The author swings a fly through this gliding run on the North Umpqua. A period of stable weather resulted in fairly low, clear water.

The author's favorite winter steelhead flies.

General Practitioner, Orange
(Esmund Drury)

Hook: *No. 4/0-2*
Tag: *Gold flat tinsel*
Tail: *Orange polar bear or similar*
Rib: *Medium gold oval*
Body: *Dubbed seal or Angora, hot orange*
Hackle: *Orange, palmered through body (or reverse palmered and bound down with rib for a more durable tie)*
Pincers: *Golden pheasant tippet feather with center removed, extending to mid-point of tail*
Wing: *(shellback) Three or four golden pheasant flank feathers veiling top of fly*
Notes: 1. For a more full-dressed version, wrap half the body, then tie in the pincers and three or four G.P. flank feathers at mid-shank; continue the body, rib and hackle forward and then tie in another batch of flank feathers at the front.

2. For Black General Practitioner, substitute all dyed-black materials except for the tail, which is black bear and the pincers, which are dyed-orange or dyed-cerise golden pheasant tippet.

3. For Purple General Practitioner, substitute purple-dyed materials and use orange-dyed or hot pink-dyed tippet feather for pincers.

Maxwell's Purple Matuka
(Forrest Maxwell)

Hook: *No. 3/0-4*
Tag: *Silver flat tinsel*
Body: *Black Angora or seal*
Rib: *Fine or medium silver oval*
Wing: *4 purple neck hackles tied Matuka style*
Collar: *Purple hackle (optional: one turn of orange or natural guinea at front)*
Note: Other variations include a silver or gold body.

Brad's Brat (Enos Bradner)

Hook: *4/0-4*
Tail: *Orange dyed golden pheasant crest*
Body: *2/5 orange, 3/5 red—seal, Angora, wool, etc.*
Rib: *Medium gold oval*
Collar: *Furnace hackle or mottled brown hen hackle*
Wing: *White topped with orange (polar bear, calf tail, dyed skunk, bucktail, etc.)*
Cheeks: *Jungle cock (optional)*

Skunk

Hook: *4/0-4*
Tag: *Silver flat tinsel*
Tail: *Red hackle fibers or red-dyed golden pheasant crest*
Rib: *Oval or flat tinsel*
Body: *Black (wool, seal fur, Angora fur, chenille, etc.)*
Hackle: *Black*
Wing: *White (polar bear, calf tail, etc.)*
Cheeks: *Jungle cock (optional)*

Dave's Redwing
(Originated by Dave McNeese)

Hook: *2/0-6, single or double*
Tail: *Golden pheasant crest feathers*
Butt: *Orange floss ribbed with fine wire*
Body: *Clumps of small scarlet hen neck feathers tied in to veil the hook on all sides*
Wing: *Two large jungle cock eyes inside two golden pheasant neck feathers (tippets)*
Cheeks: *Jungle cock eyes tied along center of wing*
Bead: *Black*

Chapter VIII

Spring Creeks

Idaho's Silver Creek offers the ultimate challenge in dry-fly angling.

Northwest fly anglers can count their good fortunes in many ways, not the least of which is the fact that several of the great spring creeks are located not much more than a day's drive from just about any point in Oregon, Washington or Idaho.

Among these productive spring creeks are the Henry's Fork and Silver Creek in Idaho, Rocky Ford Creek in Washington, the Williamson and Metolius rivers in Oregon. Of all these, the two famous Idaho spring creeks are my favorites and the favorites of many Northwest anglers.

The simple fact is that every serious fly angler should, at least once, make a pilgrimage to Silver Creek and to the Henry's Fork. These streams equate to the Mecca of our sport and represent the opportunity to experience fly fishing at its esthetic finest.

Unfortunately, the spring creeks carry with them a reputation for humbling even the most experienced anglers amongst our ranks. Certainly the wary trout of these streams can at times be very difficult, but much of their reputation is suspect nonetheless. In reality, fly anglers armed with a little knowledge of particular local hatches and a few spring-creek presentation techniques, will fare just fine on the lovely flat-water streams. Moreover, proficiency in the techniques used to present a fly to spring-creek trout cannot help but improve your success on many freestone streams and tailwaters.

What characteristics of a spring creek separate them from freestone streams? First, as their name implies, spring creeks derive most or much of their flow from spring sources rather than from snowpack and rain water. Because of this fact, a spring creek's volume of water will change little from season to season and year to year. Freestone rivers, meanwhile, commonly swell to unruly proportions during the spring and early summer and then shrink to a comparative trickle by late summer or early fall.

Also, spring creeks flow through stable streambeds whose courses change little and change slowly. Freestone rivers can change course dramatically in a single season when inundated with high water of spring runoff or major rain storms. Spring creeks also remain stable in terms of water temperature, warming and cooling only slightly and gradually, allowing trout ample time to acclimate. What's more, the typical spring creek offers ideal water temperatures for trout throughout much of the year. These spring-creek waters are also slightly alkaline compared to the relatively acidic waters of typical freestone streams.

These pH levels, along with stable water flow and temperature, allow for lush growth of rooted aquatic vegetation in the spring creeks. Visit Silver Creek or the Henry's Fork (or the other spring creeks) and you will see dense, waving masses of aquatic weeds. In turn, these plants support awesome densities of insects, including the various mayfly hatches that prompt anglers from all over to converge on the beautiful spring creeks.

Spring Creek Mayfly Hatches

Pattern choice comprises a critical element in virtually all spring-creek fishing situations and nowhere is this more evident than in the mayfly emergences. Most of the time on most of the spring-creek mayfly hatches, you will enjoy better success with floating emerger and cripple patterns than with dun patterns. This is not to say that flies tied to mimic adult mayflies will not take fish, indeed they will and at times, during certain hatches, trout will key on the duns. With many of the mayfly hatches, however, trout eat more emergers, cripples and stillborns than actual adults.

In fact, the switch from standard dry flies used on the freestone streams to the emerger and cripple patterns that fish so well on the spring creeks, represents one of the most significant adaptations a fly angler can make in terms of strategies and tactics. The same can be said of any spring-creek hatch, including the caddis and Chironomids, where pupa or downwing patterns outfish traditional flies dressed to float high and dry on the riffles and pockets of the typical Western freestone stream.

That said, let's examine the most important spring-creek mayfly hatches. In addition to the common spring-creek mayfly hatches described here, emergences of other species occur as well and might be important at a particular place and time. Those included here, however, represent the most significant of the mayfly hatches on most of our Western spring creeks.

A vibrant September day on the Henry's Fork—the largest and most famed of our Western spring creeks.

The famed green drake mayfly of the Henry's Fork and other Western spring creeks can produce some excellent early to midsummer fishing. Dave McNeese photo

I've also included a few of my favorite patterns for imitating the various mayflies, although any number of other successful patterns are available these days as well. Many excellent spring-creek patterns—the Floating Nymph, Sparkle Dun and Emergent Cripple to name a few—can be tied in whatever size and color is needed to match a specific mayfly.

Pale Morning Duns (*Ephemerella*)

The pale morning duns ("PMDs") belong to the genus *Ephemerella*. Two species are especially noted for their presence on the famous Western spring creeks: *Ephemerella inermis* and *E. infrequens*. The differences between the two are largely inconsequential to anglers. More critical is the need to simply identify a PMD hatch when one occurs.

The duns have three tails and their body color ranges from light yellow-olive to various shades of light green or even yellowish-orange. The wings are light gray. The spinner (the sexually mature adult mayfly) features clear wings and body colors ranging from the olive or brown-olive females to the rust or brownish males.

PMD hatches begin in May and last until August. They typically occur during the most comfortable time of day, with mid- to late morning through early afternoon being common. Spinner falls, which frequently induce excellent rises, occur morning, evening or both.

My favorite patterns for the PMD hatch include the PMD Emergent Cripple, the Floating Nymph, and the PMD Sparkle Dun popularized by Craig Mathews and John Juracek. Effective spinner patterns include the PMD Hackle Spinner and the Mathews/Juracek PMD Sparkle Spinner. The early-season PMDs run about a size 14. Later, size 16 and 18 flies will be needed to match the naturals.

PMD Emergent Cripple

Hook: *No. 14-18*
Tail: *Tan sparkle yarn (fine) tied as a trailing shuck*
Body: *Pale olive or pale olive-yellow dubbing (fine, such as dyed beaver or silk dubbing)*
Wings: *Z-lon or CDC, tied short and delta-style (angling to the rear from the sides of the body)*
Hackle: *Two turns of pale watery dun or light cream in front of wings, undersized by one hook size*

A swarm of white-winged blacks (*Tricorythodes* mayflies) dances above the surface of Idaho's Silver Creek.

PMD Sparkle Dun

Hook: *Dry fly, No. 14-18*
Tail: *Light brown Z-lon or similar, tied as trailing shuck*
Body: *Fine pale olive-yellow dubbing*
Wing: *Light deer hair, tied Compara-dun style*

PMD Floating Nymph

Hook: *Dry fly, No. 14-18*
Tail: *Watery dun hackle fibers*
Body: *Pale olive-yellow dubbing*
Rib: *Olive thread*
Legs: *Dun hackle fibers, short*
Wingcase: *Ball of pale gray yarn, CDC or foam*

PMD Hackle Spinner

Hook: *Dry fly, No. 14-18*
Tails: *Dun hackle fibers, divided*
Body: *Olive-tan or rust dubbing*
Rib: *Tan thread*
Wings: *Light watery dun hackle, clipped flush below and V-clipped above*

PMD Sparkle Spinner

Hook: *Dry fly, No. 14-18*
Tails: *Dun hackle fibers*
Body: *Pale rust to pale tan-olive dubbing*
Wings: *White or pale gray Z-lon or similar material*

Blue-winged Olives (*Baetis*)

Baetis mayflies, commonly known as blue-winged olives, are found on virtually all trout streams in the Northwest. The spring-creek varieties, of which there are several, produce some unbelievably dense hatches, especially early and late in the season.

Most blue-winged olives are small, with size 18-24 being common. They are readily identifiable by their highly reduced hind wings (nearly invisible to the naked eye in most species). The duns have two tails and vary in color from shades of olive to shades of gray-olive or tan. The wings are always gray. One particular *Baetis* mayfly, the tiny western olive (*B. punctiventris*), features a light green (sometimes almost chartreuse) body and very light gray—almost white—wings.

These tiny western olives typically run about a size 22-24 and their late August, early September emergence can be very dense. Any *Baetis* hatch, in fact, can be heavy enough that precise fly placement becomes critical. Trout won't move very far to eat when the water's surface is blanketed with tiny mayflies.

The best *Baetis* hatches occur during the early and late parts of the season and the heaviest emergences frequently coincide with overcast, cool weather. So exceptional can foul-weather *Baetis* hatches be, that veteran spring-creek anglers generally start drooling at the onset of drizzle, wind and approaching cold fronts. At these times, the *Baetis* duns ride the water for many yards before their wings are dry enough for flight—thus making easy pickings for trout.

Most of the time my favorite blue-winged olive pattern is a Floating Nymph. Trout generally seem to prefer the emerging dun as it struggles in the surface film. The Emergent Cripple pattern is effective, as well, due to the high number of stillborns and cripples accompanying any *Baetis* hatch. Other good patterns include the Compara-dun and the Sparkle Dun.

Baetis Floating Nymph

Hook: *Dry fly, No. 16-24 (commonly 18-22)*
Tail: *Light dun hackle fibers*
Body: *Fine dubbing to match natural: olive, pale olive, olive-tan*
Wingcase: *Ball of gray dubbing, CDC or foam*
Legs: *Light dun hackle fibers, short*

Baetis Emergent Cripple

Hook: *Dry fly, No. 18-22*
Tail: *Fine sparkle yarn tied as trailing shuck (sparse)*
Body: *Fine dubbing to match natural (olive, pale olive, olive-tan, etc.)*
Wings: *Fine gray sparkle yarn or gray CDC, tied short, spent and delta-style*
Legs: *One turn of dun hackle on larger sizes only*

The author with a nice brown trout from a small spring creek in the Rockies. In addition to the famous streams, small little-known spring creeks meander across valleys and farmlands throughout the West. Al Shewey photo

Effective mayfly patterns for spring-creek fishing.

Baetis Sparkle Dun

Hook: *Dry fly, No. 16-20*
Tail: *Tan sparkle yarn as trailing shuck*
Body: *Olive, olive-tan, pale-olive*
Wing: *Deer hair tied Compara-dun style*
Note: *Baetis Compara-dun is identical except the tail is dun hackle fibers, tied short and divided*

Green Drakes

Among the most popular of spring-creek mayflies are the stately green drakes, especially the large *Drunella grandis*, which offers some very good hatches on the Henry's Fork during June. As their name suggests, the green drakes are predominantly green, featuring attractive yellow highlights. The wings are gray. The duns sport three tails and robust bodies.

Drunella grandis is a large mayfly, its imitations being tied on No. 10-12 hooks. Smaller versions are common as well, especially the slate-winged olive (*D. flavilinea*), which hatches on the Henry's Fork during July. Nearly identical in color to the big green drake, the slate-winged olive (sometimes called "small western green drake" or simply "*flav*") is more along the lines of a size 14.

The big green drakes emerge sometime between late morning and early afternoon on the Henry's Fork. During July, the slate-winged olives emerge during late afternoon or evening.

For the big green drakes, I fish a Floating Emerger or an Emergent Cripple. The exception to this is when I clearly observe that a particular trout is eating the duns. Then I switch to a Para-drake. For the *flavs*, I prefer a Floating Nymph or Sparkle Dun.

Green Drake Emergent Cripple

Hook: *Dry fly, No. 10-14*
Tail: *Brown sparkle yarn tied as trailing shuck*
Body: *Olive green with light green thread for a rib*
Wings: *Gray sparkle yarn or Z-lon, tied short, spent and delta-style*
Legs: *2 turns of dyed olive grizzly hackle, undersized*

Flavilinea Floating Nymph

Hook: *Dry fly, No. 14*
Tail: *Dun hackle fibers, short*
Body: *Olive-green dubbing ribbed with light olive thread*
Wingcase: *Ball of gray dubbing, CDC or foam*
Legs: *Dun hackle fibers, short*

Flavilinea Sparkle Dun

Hook: *Dry fly, No. 14*
Tail: *Tan Z-lon or similar tied as trailing shuck*
Body: *Olive-green dubbing ribbed with green thread*
Wing: *Deer hair tied Compara-dun style*

Green Drake Para-drake (Mike Lawson)

Hook: *Dry fly, No. 10-14*
Tails: *Dark moose hairs*
Body: *Elk hair dyed dark olive, tied extended using chartreuse thread*
Wing: *Dark gray deer hair tied as post*
Hackle: *Chartreuse-dyed grizzly saddle, tied parachute*

Tricos (White-winged Blacks)

The *Tricos*, or white-winged blacks (*Tricorythodes*), comprise one of the most important and enjoyable of the late-summer mayfly hatches on Silver Creek and on the Henry's Fork. The "trikes" hatch in the morning, with the spinner fall occurring almost simultaneously.

The *Trico* duns are easily identifiable by their small size and their white wings. They have only one pair of wings (no hind wings) and three tails. Male duns are otherwise black; females, olive. Spinners have clear wings, but are otherwise similar in color. Size 18 through 22 imitations will match the naturals.

Spinner patterns (my favorite is the *Trico* Hackle Spinner) produce well throughout the hatch/spinner fall most of the time. At times, at least on certain trout, an ant or beetle pattern will work better than a fly that mimics the hordes of *Tricos* adrift on the surface. See "Chasing the Best Hatches" (page 39) for my two favorite *Trico* patterns.

Callibaetis (Speckled-Wing Dun)

Primarily known as a mayfly of lakes, ponds and reservoirs, the speckled-wing duns offer good hatches on the slow, weedy sections of the Henry's Fork and on the backwater portions of Silver Creek. These hatches occur during late summer afternoons, starting as early as 10 a.m. or as late as 3 p.m.

The *Callibaetis* is a rather large mayfly for late summer, with size 14 and 16 imitations usually necessary. As its common name might suggest, this mayfly is distinguished by its heavily patterned wings. The duns have two tails and range in color from pale gray to light tan to pale olive or olive-tan.

Callibaetis spinners, which sometimes appear about the same time as the emergence, feature clear wings with slight brownish mottling. The body color of the spinners often corresponds to that of the dun except that in the spinner stage you may observe a more pronounced difference in shade between the insect's back and its underside.

Only on occasion will the speckled-wing dun emerge in dense numbers. More common are sparse hatches wherein the duns appear in scattered bunches, often coming and going in relatively thin waves. The duns tend to ride the water for several feet before flying off, so trout can eat them readily. If spinners are present, trout eat them right along with the duns.

I've had especially good fishing with sparkle duns and emergent cripples during the *Callibaetis* hatch. Other effective patterns include Compara-duns and Troth Gulper Specials.

Callibaetis Emergent Cripple
Hook: *Dry fly, No. 14-16*
Tail: *Tan sparkle yarn tied as trailing shuck*
Body: *Tan or tannish olive dubbing*
Wings: *Gray-brown Z-lon or similar, tied short, spent and delta style*
Hackle: *Two turns of light dun*

Callibaetis Sparkle Dun
Hook: *Dry fly, No. 14-16*
Tail: *Pale gray Z-lon or similar tied as a trailing shuck*
Body: *Tan dubbing*
Wing: *Gray deer hair, tied Compara-dun style*

Callibaetis Gulper Special (Al Troth)
Hook: *Dry fly, No. 14-16*
Tail: *Grizzly hackle fibers (divided is optional)*
Body: *Tan or pale olive-tan dubbing*
Wing: *Gray poly yarn tied as post*
Hackle: *A few turns of grizzly hackle, parachute style*

This beautiful rainbow took an ant pattern fished below an overhanging bank on the Henry's Fork.

The smooth, clear water of spring creeks demands that anglers approach trout with stealth.

Mahogany Dun (*Paraleptophlebia*)

The mahogany dun, a late-season mayfly especially prominent on the Henry's Fork, offers some fine fishing during September. Mahogany duns are indeed a rich chocolate brown in color, with gray wings. They run about a size 16. During a good hatch, the mahogany dun emergence will span a period of several hours, typically beginning mid- to late morning and lasting until early or mid- afternoon.

These hatches are sporadic in nature, rarely, if ever, as dense as the *Baetis* hatches that occur the same time of year. The duns often arrive in sparse waves. This arrangement is to the angler's advantage because trout will travel a foot or more to get to a dun or emerging nymph. Moreover, trout seem to relish these mayflies, after all, the mahogany duns are the largest mayflies left by the time mid-September arrives.

I generally fish my Mahogany Emerger pattern. This fly, or another surface-film emerger, will generally outfish dun imitations. Other effective flies include the Sparkle Dun, Floating Pheasant Tail Nymph, Emergent Cripple and mahogany-colored floating nymphs. See "Chasing the Best Hatches" for dressings.

Other Mayflies

Various Northwest spring creeks also host mayfly emergences in addition to those discussed. These include brown drakes (*Ephemera*); gray drakes (*Siphlonurus*); *Hexagenia limbata*, the giant yellow mayfly of the Williamson River; Sulpher duns (*Centroptilum*) of the Paradise Valley spring creeks near Livingston, Montana; several more-or-less freestone varieties of mayflies found on the Metolius and on certain sections of other streams. For more details on these hatches, which can be significant on their host streams, refer to *Mastering the Spring Creeks* and *The Complete Book of Western Hatches* (Frank Amato Publications, Inc.).

Spring Creek Terrestrials

Terrestrial insects—primarily ants, beetles and hoppers—form an important ingredient in the diet of many spring-creek trout. On Northwest spring creeks, these insects become especially important from midsummer through early or mid-autumn.

At times, in fact, terrestrial insects can be so abundant in the drift that certain trout become selective to particular ants or beetles, sometimes even hoppers. This situation is most evident on the Henry's Fork (and other spring creeks) during August and early September when the occasional horde of flying ants is blown onto the water's surface. In addition, some trout take up feeding positions along the bank where they feed almost exclusively on terrestrials.

A selection of terrestrial patterns should always be at hand when you venture to the spring creeks. Basic patterns, such as fur ants and peacock beetles, will prove effective most of the time. Quite some time ago, I settled on the McMurray Fur Ant as my favorite ant pattern. The McMurray Ant is a dressing featuring a pre-formed, lacquered balsa-wood body comprised of two separate segments strung on a tiny section of fairly stiff monofilament. These pre-formed bodies are available at some fly shops, especially in the Rockies. To tie the McMurray Fur Ant, simply cut the front segment away and attach the rear segment to the rear of the hook. Add

The downstream cast is critical to consistent success on spring creeks. Here an angler on Silver Creek slides the fly into the exact feeding lane . . .

two turns of hackle and wings if desired, then form a head of spun fur.

Tim Blount and I have had exceptionally success with this pattern when trout get difficult. Most of the time, however, a sparsely dressed fur ant will do the trick. Beetle patterns and hopper patterns, whichever specific dressing you choose, should likewise be tied sparse: Trout living in the smooth waters of spring creeks have ample opportunity to inspect a fly and they often turn away from a heavily-dressed terrestrial.

Spring Creek Caddisflies and Chironomids

Both caddisflies and Chironomids can be of significance on spring creeks. Caddisflies provide some exceptional fishing, so long as you take the time to first determine whether the trout are taking emerging caddis or ovipositing caddis. A river full of rising trout and yet seemingly devoid of insects on the surface frequently indicates a caddis emergence: The adults escape almost immediately upon reaching the surface, so the trout feed on pupae just below or in the film. The result is lots of rises but no floating insects.

During cool weather, and with certain caddis species, the adults may drift on the surface for a time and are then eaten right along with the pupae. The key is to identify whether a certain trout is feeding on pupae or adults and then choose the appropriate imitation.

On the other hand, many caddis species deposit their eggs on the surface and then fall spent on the water. Trout are quick to take advantage of such an easy meal, especially when large numbers of insects are on the water. These spent caddis are generally easy to imitate with a downwing pattern such as Mike Lawson's Spent Partridge Caddis or Carl Richards' Quad-wing Caddis.

Chironomids are perhaps easier to figure out than caddisflies. Most of the time, trout eat the pupae, either at the surface or just under the surface. Generally speaking, only cold days offer the trout much opportunity to feed on adult "midges."

A floating Chironomid pupa or "emerger" pattern will usually outperform an imitation of the winged adult.

However, if you clearly see that a particular trout is eating adults, switch to a Griffith's Gnat or another imitation of the adult midge.

Undoubtedly, the most difficult part of fishing Chironomids is dealing with the tiny size of the naturals. Spring-creek Chironomids must often be imitated with size 22-24 hooks, sometimes smaller still. If you have trouble seeing your fly on the water, attach a small dry fly as a dropper some 18 inches above the midge pattern. This dry fly (I generally use a size 18 or 20 Griffith's Gnat) serves as your locater, allowing you to follow the approximate drift of the lead fly.

For more information about both Chironomids and caddis as they relate to spring-creek fishing, see *Mastering the Spring Creeks*.

Techniques For Spring-Creek Fishing

Perhaps the biggest factor affecting the success of a fly angler on the flat-water streams is his or her ability to change from the freestone-stream techniques most of us grew up with to the more stealthful approach needed to assure consistent prosperity on the spring creeks. Moreover, if you understand a little about how spring-creek trout live and feed, you will be better able to devise effective methods for dealing with these trout.

Let's tackle the latter concept first. Spring-creek trout live in a world of comparative leisure. Where a trout residing in a tumbling riffle must make quick decisions about what to eat and what not to eat, its counterpart on a smooth spring-creek can examine potential prey in detail. What's more, a fast-water trout is frequently too inundated by the hustle and bustle of hurrying currents to know when an angler is within casting range. Put that same trout under the mirror-like surface of a spring creek, and it can detect danger from quite a distance. Finally, a spring-creek trout has the luxury of holding just inches below the surface during a hatch, sipping from a massive parade of insects. A trout of the riffles and runs of a freestone stream must hold near the bottom, where currents are cushioned, and make calculated dashes to the surface to eat drifting insects.

All of these factors and more determine the methods used by successful spring-creek anglers. You might

. . . and then lowers the rod tip to enact a drag-free drift.

choose to cast upstream and across to a trout holding in the riffles of a freestone river. On the flat waters of our popular Western spring creeks, however, a downstream cast is often needed to fool wary, selective trout. The downstream angle allows the fish to view the fly first, with the line and leader never drifting through the trout's "window" of vision.

Before you can even cast, however, you must put yourself in a position to make the best possible presentation. This usually means getting close. In fact, some of the most useful casting and mending techniques applied by spring-creek anglers are predicated by the fact that the angler will be as close as possible to the trout.

Finally, spring-creek anglers must possess a basic understanding of spring-creek trout foods and which flies best imitate them. On freestone streams all over the West we could catch a lot of trout on a size 12 Royal Wulff. But that fly or the many other general-use attractor patterns won't be of much use during a heavy spring-creek hatch of pale morning duns. Sure, there are times when a particular spring-creek trout or several trout willingly accept a fly that doesn't seem to match much of anything; most of time, though, spring-creek anglers must be serious students of matching the hatch.

What follows is an abbreviated guide to the basic principles of spring-creek fishing. At the risk of being redundant, I will again point out that anyone who wishes to get serious about tackling the Western spring creeks will find *Mastering the Spring Creeks* a valuable guide. Ask for a copy at your local fly shop or bookstore, or contact Frank Amato Publications. Now for some basic principles that will improve success on the spring creeks:

1. Know what hatches to expect when you visit a particular spring creek. In other words, do your homework. Read whatever literature is available on a particular stream and call the fly shops in that area. This way you can anticipate the hatches and be on the stream at the right time with the right flies.

2. Carry all the flies you expect you might need. Although you might time your trip to coincide with one of the major

A guide watches intently as his client casts to a rising trout on Silver Creek.

An angler plays a nice rainbow hooked during the *Trico* hatch on Idaho's Silver Creek.

mayfly hatches, bear in mind that hatches can be fleeting affairs and that the one you are counting on may or may not provide the best fishing of the day. So be prepared to fish any other hatch that can occur at the same time of year and also carry a selection of terrestrial patterns and nymphs that might be needed.

3. Figure out what the trout are eating. Compound hatches, wherein two or more species of insect occupy the drift simultaneously, are common affairs on spring creeks. Often, these take the form of what we call "masking hatches," which occur when a larger and/or more obvious insect overshadows the smaller insects on which the trout are feeding. On still other occasions, trout rise even though you see nothing on the water. Caddis hatches and some mayfly spinner falls often cause these situations; other times, small ants or beetles, floating low in the surface film, are responsible.

In any case, expect to spend a fair amount of time not knowing for certain what trout are eating. Close observation, coupled with liberal use of a mesh sampling net, will keep these guessing games to a minimum. Most of us go with trial and error first, casting a fly we think might work. Only after countless refusals do we realize we need to observe more closely and perhaps sample the drift with our handy mesh net.

Always bear in mind that individual trout may be feeding on different insects at the same time. In other words, just because you see a river full of rising trout, don't automatically assume that all the trout are feeding on the same bug or on the same stage of an emergence. Each time you approach a particular trout, you must begin anew the task of determining what food that fish is eating. Naturally, if you are fishing over a dense hatch of one particular insect and you have already taken several fish on a like imitation, you can feel reasonably certain that the next rising trout you approach will also be eating that particular bug. Once in a while, however, spring-creek trout throw you a curve: in the midst of a heavy hatch of *Baetis* mayflies, for example, you find a single trout ignoring the mayflies in favor of ants and beetles awash in the drift.

The reach cast, illustrated here, is an important technique for spring creek anglers . ...

4. Choose the appropriate imitation. If you do your homework on the hatches you expect to encounter, and combine this research with close observation, fly choice won't pose too much of a problem most of the time. If, for example, you have learned that a Pale Morning Dun Floating Nymph generally works better than a dun imitation, you will know which pattern to choose at the onset of that hatch. Only if direct observation confirms that a particular trout is eating the PMD duns would you choose a like imitation.

5. Get close to the fish. Many of the presentation techniques used on spring-creek trout depend upon the angler's close proximity to the trout—in many cases within 30 feet; if possible, within 20 feet. Obviously, close approach requires stealth. Wade slowly and quietly, use all available cover to conceal your approach; keep an eye on your shadow.

On Silver Creek and on parts of the Henry's Fork, trout have become so conditioned to the inevitable presence of wading anglers, the fish simply continue feeding despite the fact that they know you are there. They continue feeding, however, with a renewed selectivity. The best way to combat these devils is to treat every trout and every pod of trout as if the fish are wild and timid. In other words, select your route of approach with care and then wade with great stealth, slowly and quietly. Once you gain the position from which you intend to cast, stand still for several minutes. Any time you detect a change in the trout's feeding pattern or intensity during your approach, stop and wait for a time. Once the fish resumes feeding normally, continue your approach.

6. Learn, practice and apply the downstream presentation. For most spring-creek trout the best casting position is one that allows you to deliver the fly downstream. By casting downstream, you can first dead-drift the fly over the fish and then slide the line away from the trout's feeding lane in preparation for another cast. This technique of sliding the fly and line away from the trout's feeding lane is aptly called the "slide method."

Incidentally, the term "feeding lane" refers to that portion of the current where the fish is actively feeding at a given time. During a dense hatch, when countless insects cover the water, trout can find ample food by simply holding in one spot and feeding from an area just a few inches wide. During a more sparse drift of insects, a trout might have to patrol a feeding lane two or three feet wide in order to find enough to eat. By watching a trout rise several times, you will get an idea of how far to the left or right that fish will move to take an insect. Then you have an idea about the width of that trout's feeding lane. Naturally, in spring-creek fishing, it is imperative that the angler place his or her fly directly in the trout's feeding lane.

The slide method is an easy way to place the fly in the feeding lane and at the same time avoid having the line and leader float over the fish. Naturally, an accurate initial cast into the feeding lane is the ideal way to begin the presentation. If you miss, however, your upstream (and slightly off to one side) position allows you to slide the fly into the correct current lane. After lifting the rod to slide the fly into position, immediately lower the tip and perhaps shake extra line out of the guides in order to assure a drag-free drift.

Again, an accurate cast in the first place often allows for a better presentation. From the upstream position, you can use a reach cast to first place the fly into the feeding lane and then provide slack for the drift. To perform the reach cast, simply reach your arm and rod upstream just as the line straightens on the forestroke. Ideally, the fly will land three or four feet upstream from the trout, at which time you need only reach your rod tip downstream toward the fly to provide enough slack line for a drag-free drift of several feet. If the fly drifts beyond the trout unmolested, swing the rod slowly over to the other side of your body to slide the line and leader out of the trout's field of vision, then pick up for the next cast. A spring-creek trout, especially during a heavy hatch, might require dozens of casts before rising to the fly.

Another useful downstream cast is the "stop cast," or "bounce cast." To accomplish the stop cast, deliver a normal backstroke and then stop the rod abruptly, rather high, on the forestroke, causing the line to rebound toward you and land on the water in a series of curves. With a little practice, you can deliver a "straight-line stop cast," which eliminates the curves in the line but allows you to provide a short, drag-free drift simply by lowering the rod tip.

Less accurate, but still useful at times for downstream presentations, is the "wiggle" or "serpentine" cast. To execute the serpentine cast, wiggle the rod tip side to side with gentle but firm wrist motions as the line straightens on the forestroke. The result will be a series of S-curves in the line. These curves will help absorb current seams before they cause the fly to drag.

Another of the so-called slack-line casts, the "parachute cast," is probably the least accurate of all these techniques. Nonetheless, the parachute cast proves valuable at times. It is performed by tilting the entire casting plane slightly backward so the forestroke is driven into the air rather than parallel with the water. Upon completion of the forestroke, the line falls limply to the water in a series of loose curves.

No matter which cast you employ, the drift of the fly is easier to control if you can avoid casting across multiple current speeds. Therefore, position yourself within a rod's length laterally of the trout's position and as far upstream as needed to avoid spooking your quarry. Situating yourself within a rod's length laterally of the trout's position allows you to control the exact drift of the fly: You can slide the fly into the exact feeding lane and you can slide the fly to the side for the next cast.

Indeed, if you take the time to learn these downstream presentation techniques, your success on rivers like the Henry's Fork, Silver Creek, Rocky Ford Creek and the Metolius will improve dramatically. What's more, the downstream presentation will prove valuable in many instances on your favorite freestone streams, thus making you a more efficient and able fly angler.

I have always believed that every dedicated fly angler deserves to fish the famous Western spring creeks at some time in his or her angling life. Unfortunately, the reputations that go along with these streams—super-smart, super-difficult trout and the supposed need to be a master entomologist to expect success—tend to scare some anglers away from what might well be the most rewarding of fly fishing experiences. Forget those hyped-up reputations. Just follow the guidelines outlined above and I think you will find places like Silver Creek and the Henry's Fork to be nothing short of exquisitely enjoyable.

. . . allowing for very precise placement of the fly line.

Chapter IX

Nymphing the Northwest

Classic pocket water like this section of the McKenzie River east of Eugene, Oregon, offers excellent prospects for nymphing.

I'd been waiting for the phone call for a couple of weeks. Dave Tucker, owner of Streamside Adventures in Boise, assured me he would call the minute the crappie bite picked up out on Brownlee Reservoir. Mid-May came and went with no word. The first week in June came and I knew the crappie action had to get underway at any time. Still no phone call, but I had penciled in Brownlee for the next weekend anyway.

I left for a speaking engagement on a Thursday morning, returning home Friday afternoon. Dee was at work, but she had left a note from the day before. Tucker had called and disappointment rained on my parade: Dee's note read, "Dave Tucker called—crappy fishing right now."

Well, what the hell. I figured I could find something to do with my weekend, even though crappie wouldn't be involved. I decided on the McKenzie, figuring a few big rainbows might help me forget about those crappie for a while. I left a note for Dee and headed for Eugene.

The next morning, unfortunately, I couldn't buy a rise on the lower McKenzie. Few bugs graced the surface all day so eventually I quit waiting for hatches and decided to try dredging a few fish out with nymphs. This turned out to be one of the better decisions I'd made that week, as several nice trout and a dozen or so whitefish came to the net.

Perhaps it wasn't as pretty or as riveting as dry-fly fishing, but I likely wouldn't have risen a trout all day had I stuck with dries. That's nymphing in a nutshell: Competence in fishing nymphs on a variety of waters allows anglers to take fish even on those days when nothing stirs on the surface and when no floating attractor pattern in the box can bring a trout up from the depths.

So it may not have been the ideal day on the McKenzie, but at least I was fishing. Sure I'd rather have been hammering crappie and smallmouth on Brownlee, but I'd be there just as soon as Tucker sent word that the bite was on.

I returned home that Saturday night. I hadn't seen Dee in three days and the first thing she said was, "Did you get the note I left?"

"Yeah, I saw it before I left—that's why I went to the McKenzie," I answered.

"But I thought you wanted to catch crappie and the guy who called said it was good right now."

That's when it hit me. Dee's usually competent spelling skills had faltered a bit. I told her as much: "Crappy fishing right now." I showed her the note she had written. Her face went blank for a few seconds and then she started laughing. She's been laughing about that one ever since.

Nymphing Skills For the Northwest Angler

Most successful nymph fishing can be summarized in three basic concepts: 1. Get the flies on or near the bottom; 2. Control the drift in a manner that allows you to detect strikes quickly and easily; 3. Use patterns that catch fish and in which you have confidence.

We'll tackle the last of these first, that being the question of which nymph patterns to choose. Essentially, we can divide nymphs into two broad categories. The first of these groupings includes the basic attractor types—patterns that look edible to the fish but which don't necessarily imitate a particular insect. Examples include the ever-useful Gold Ribbed Hare's Ear, Pheasant Tail Nymph and Zug Bug.

The other category of nymphs is composed of patterns designed to mimic particular insects like stoneflies, caddis larvae or specific mayflies. Examples from this exhaustive category include some of my favorites like the Brook's Stonefly Nymph, Peeking Caddis, Green Rockworm and Green Drake Nymph. Some of these imitative patterns, like the Peeking Caddis and Brook's Stone, can be tied in a variety of sizes and shades to represent different caddis larvae and stonefly nymphs, respectively.

Others, however, are designed to match certain insects as closely as possible. The Lawson Green Drake Nymph, for example, generally need only be tied on size 10-12 hooks to match the green drake nymphs found in most streams. Similarly, the Green Rockworm, when used specifically to represent any of several free-living caddis, rarely needs to be tied in more than one shade and two or three sizes.

Given the profusion of nymph patterns, some of which fit either category depending on the situation in which they are fished, how do you choose which flies to rely on day in and day out? Every experienced angler has some favorite general use patterns—flies that consistently take fish on a variety of streams. My favorites are pretty standard among nymph anglers: Hare's Ear Nymph, Pheasant Tail Nymph, Zug Bug, Brook's Stone, Soft-Hackle Zug Bug, Peeking Caddis. Tied in a variety of sizes and shades, patterns from this list will catch trout in any stream.

In fact, that selection of flies accounts for the vast majority of trout I take on nymphs while fishing freestone streams. Add to that list a few patterns that work well on particular waters and I'm in business. If I fish a river or section of river where a particular insect predominates—perhaps free-living caddis on the Deschutes, golden stone nymphs on parts of the Snake or scuds on some of my favorite desert streams—then I naturally employ appropriate imitations.

Like many serious "nymphers," I usually fish two or three flies at a time, each spaced eight to 14 inches apart on the tippet. A typical setup on many of our freestone rivers would feature a Brook's Stonefly Nymph followed by some combination of Hare's Ear Nymphs, Pheasant Tails, Zug Bugs and Peeking Caddis. Often I start with a size 10 or 12 Hare's Ear and a size 12 or 14 Pheasant Tail Nymph along with a size 8 Brook's Stone. If I fish a river dominated by mayflies, I might rig a series of small Pheasant Tail Nymphs or a Hare's Ear and a pair of Pheasant Tails.

Getting Flies On the Bottom

As of this writing, one of fly fishing's many mini-trends—the bead-head craze—has swept across the nymph-fishing community. Fly anglers rave about the effectiveness of these new bead-head nymphs, about how they outfish the traditional nymphs. We have Bead-head Hare's Ears, Bead-head Pheasant Tails, Bead-head Zug Bugs and Bead-head everything else.

So are these bead-head flies really more effective than standard dressings? In a way, yes. Because of the jig-like heads on these bead-head flies, people are finally getting flies on the bottom where they will catch fish. In my teaching fly-fishing schools over the years, I have noticed that most beginning anglers really don't realize how critical is this idea of getting nymphs on the bottom in a freestone stream. Moreover, even if they understand the inherent importance of doing so, many anglers don't know how to get flies on the bottom and fish them there or they assume their nymphs are drifting along the bottom when in fact they are not.

I would argue, then, that the effectiveness of the bead-head nymphs lies primarily, if not wholly, in the ability of these flies to sink quickly to the bottom even in the hands of an angler who does everything wrong, so to speak. Thus the bead-head flies teach us a valuable lesson about nymphing: Get the flies on the bottom and keep them there through the drift.

In the hands of an angler who can do just that, standard nymphs prove just as effective as bead-head nymphs. With standard nymphs, we must weight the flies with lead wire or attach split shot to the leader, or both. One of the advantages of using a multiple-fly setup, in fact, is that at least one of the flies can be extra-heavily weighted (e.g. a big, heavily-leaded Stonefly Nymph). Like a split shot, this super-heavy nymph will drag the other flies to the bottom; unlike a split shot, this big, heavy nymph might well be eaten by a trout.

When rainstorms blew out this small desert stream, the author abandoned unsuccessful dry flies in favor of nymphs and caught several trout during what otherwise would have been a fishless outing.

In deep, heavy water, you may still need split shot. Split shot causes two problems: First, all but the tiniest shot casts about as well as half a watermelon; second, split shot often hangs up on the bottom and can cost you a lot of flies, especially with two- and three-fly rigs.

Luckily, we rarely need cast too far when nymphing and a slightly opened casting stroke—sometimes more like a lob than a cast—will prevent you from bouncing split shot off the back of your skull. As for hanging up on the bottom, I found long ago that the best way to prevent the loss of a lot of flies is to attach the split shot at strategic points. Frequently, I will attach an extra few inches of tippet below the lead fly and pinch a shot onto the end, below all the flies. Otherwise, I generally tie a blood knot on the leader between two of the flies and then attach the split shot to a tag end protruding from this knot. With either method, the idea is to enable the split shot to slide off the monofilament before the tippet breaks as you pull to free a snag.

Naturally, things don't always work out as planned. Losing flies is part of the nymph-fishing game. Despite this unfortunate fact, I still use three flies at a time. I believe three flies give me three times the chance that a trout will grab one of the flies.

For quite a few years, I attached my dropper flies by tying them to tag ends left from blood knots. By keeping these dropper flies suspended just an inch or so from the main tippet,

Nymphing often proves effective when surface tactics fail. Such was the case on this mountain stream in Oregon.

I seldom had tangles. Despite the effectiveness of this method, I now tie the nymphs "in-line" by attaching the tippet from the hook bend of one fly to the eye of the following fly. Although tangles occur at about the same frequency as with my older method, the in-line rigging assembles faster and appears to be somewhat stronger under the weight of a big trout.

With either method, I space the flies only eight to 14 inches apart. Also, I typically attach the heaviest fly as the top dropper, higher up on the leader than the other flies. My thinking is that the heavier fly will help sink the smaller patterns, dragging them to the bottom.

What's more, I use light tippet, which cuts through the surface tension quickly and easily. If a large stonefly is to be my top dropper, I begin with a nine-foot, 4X leader. First I attach the Stonefly Nymph. Then, using an improved clinch knot, I tie about 16 inches of 5X material to the hook bend of the Stonefly Nymph. On the other end of this length of 5X, I attach one of the smaller flies. Then I repeat the process, again using 5X material, to attach a lead fly below the second nymph.

If I am using only small nymphs, I begin with a nine-foot or 12-foot 5X leader and then add sections of 5X or even 6X (with size 16-20 patterns) to attach the two bottom flies. The long, light tippets penetrate the surface far more quickly than the typical 7-1/2-foot, 3X or 4X leaders recommended for nymph fishing in years past. Certainly 3X or 4X tippet would save a few flies from a watery grave, but I'm not in this game to worry over a few lost flies.

Fishing the Nymphs

One more piece of tackle will complete your nymphing setup, the strike indicator. Many items can serve as strike indicators, ranging from pieces of stick-on foam and hollowed out sections of bright-colored fly line to sections of bright yarn and even dry flies tied well up the leader. My favorite, however, and these days the choice of many nymph anglers, is the Corkie, which is a little hard-foam ball used for drift-fishing.

The Corkie's primary advantage lies in the fact that you can move it up and down the leader, depending on the depth and speed of the water you are fishing. In a three-foot-deep, slow riffle, place the Corkie four feet above the lead fly. Walk downstream to a fast, four-foot-deep chute and you can easily move the Corkie a couple of feet up the leader. I use a wood toothpick to hold the Corkie in place: Slide the Corkie to the appropriate place on the leader, jam a toothpick into the hole until the Corkie is firmly in place and break off the toothpick. When you need to move the Corkie, loosen the toothpick, slide the indicator into a new position and then jam the toothpick into place again.

Incidentally, more and more anglers have taken to the practice of simply placing the strike indicator on the leader butt just below its juncture with the fly line. While this arrangement will generally prove effective, I prefer to keep the indicator as close as possible to the flies. By doing this I can detect the strike (by any sudden movement of the indicator) a fraction of a second earlier than if the Corkie is placed another few feet up the leader. In other words, the further up the leader you place the indicator, the further the energy from the trout's strike must transmit up the leader before you see the Corkie twitch.

In any case, having rigged your nymphing setup for maximum efficiency, you must now present the flies in a manner that gets them down to the trout's level. Start by wading in at the downstream extent of a "trouty-looking" riffle or run. Cast the flies upstream and somewhat across. As the nymphs sink, mend the line, but not the leader, slightly upstream. This mend is intended to prevent the fly line from drifting downstream too far ahead of the flies. If the fly line accelerates downstream ahead of the leader, the flies will be pulled away from the bottom. However, you want the leader to remain directly above or slightly downstream of the drifting flies, allowing for solid hookups when the trout, facing upstream, grabs the fly.

Now watch your indicator. As the indicator drifts in front of your position, raise the rod tip to remove some of the slack line from the surface. Then, as the indicator drifts past your position, begin lowering the rod tip and reaching the rod downstream. At the downstream extent of the presentation, shake slack line out the rod tip to extend the drift several more feet.

The general idea is to keep reasonably direct contact with the flies throughout the drift. By doing so, you can set the hook quickly at any sign of a strike (when the indicator twitches or stops suddenly). This method of raising and lowering the rod tip to help maintain contact with the flies has been dubbed "high-sticking."

High-sticking, however, is not the only method of fishing nymphs. Another technique is to allow slack line to drift along above the flies while you keep your rod tip close to the water's surface. If the indicator twitches or stops, immediately (and smoothly) jerk the rod downstream to set the hook. Because you are keeping the rod tip low, this quick, smooth movement of the rod transfers quickly through the line and sets the hook in the corner of the trout's mouth. While high-sticking is frequently the method of choice for close-in fishing, especially with big, heavy nymphs, this latter method is more effective for long-line presentations.

In either case, be sure to cast far enough upstream to allow the flies to reach the bottom ahead of the target area. Then use whatever line mends are needed to allow for a long, drag-free drift. In time, you will learn to differentiate between strikes from trout and hesitations caused by flies or split shot catching on rocks underwater. In fact, if you can train yourself to set the hook gently, without jerking the flies right out of the water every time the indicator moves, you can fish right through those bothersome momentary snags when the fly grabs hold of a rock just long enough to move the Corkie.

Finally, cover the water thoroughly when fishing nymphs. Allow eight or ten drifts for each small area before stepping upstream. Of course the size of the stream will dictate how many casts you make to a given area. After all, a big riffle in the Deschutes demands far more drifts than a yard-long pocket behind a boulder in a high-mountain stream.

Brook's Stonefly Nymph

Hook: *3XL or 4XL nymph, No. 4-8*
Tail: *Black or brown biots*
Body: *Black wool yarn*
Rib: *Copper wire*
Legs: *Two turns of mixed grizzly and brown hackle, fairly sparse*

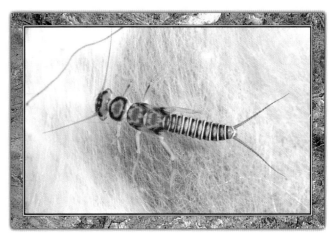

A golden stonefly nymph. Many stonefly nymphs, including the goldens, form a staple in the diet of trout residing in freestone rivers throughout the West. Dave McNeese photo

Gold Ribbed Hare's Ear Nymph

Hook: *2XL or 3XL wet fly or nymph, No. 6-16*
Tail: *Partridge fibers*
Body: *Hare's mask fur, dubbed*
Rib: *Fine gold oval*
Wingcase: *Dark turkey or Krystal Flash*

Pheasant Tail Nymph (Frank Sawyer)

Hook: *2XL or 3XL wet fly or nymph, No. 8-18*
Tail: *Pheasant tail fibers*
Abdomen: *Pheasant tail fibers wrapped up shank*
Rib: *Fine copper wire, counterwrapped*
Thorax: *Peacock herl*
Wingcase: *Pheasant tail fibers*
Legs: *Pheasant tail fibers (same bunch as wingcase folded back under fly)*

Peeking Caddis (George Anderson)

Hook: *2XL or 3XL nymph, No. 6-16*
Case: *Natural dark hare's ear fur*
Rib: *Fine gold or copper wire or oval*
Body: *Two turns of olive or cream dubbing*
Legs: *Brown partridge or grouse*
Head: *Black ostrich herl*

Brassie (Gene Lynch)

Hook: *Wet fly or nymph, No. 12-20*
Body: *Copper wire (also tied with red or green-colored wire)*
Head: *Black fur, ostrich, or peacock herl*

Girdle Bug

Hook: *3XL nymph, No. 4-10*
Tail: *Two white rubber legs*
Legs: *Three pairs of white rubber legs*
Body: *Black chenille*

Zug Bug (Cliff Zug)

Hook: *2XL or 3XL wet fly, No. 8-16*
Tail: *Peacock sword fibers*
Body: *Peacock herl*
Rib: *Fine silver or gold oval*
Throat: *Brown hackle fibers or brown partridge fibers*
Wingcase: *Lemon wood duck, tied in at front and trimmed at mid-body*

Chapter X

Pike, Catfish, Carp and other Northwest Myths and Legends

In the author's experience, carp tend to eat flies only when you fish in earnest for other elusive species. Try to fish for carp on purpose and you'll likely never see one.

I've never met a fish I wouldn't fish for, but I've met a few I might think twice about before pursuing them on a regular basis.

Take for example the toothy beast known as the northern pike. From what little I've seen, a northern pike is hardly more than a belligerent snake with fins and big, sharp teeth. Of course I haven't seen many of them. One to be exact. If not for Brent Snow, I'd have never seen even that one pike. Thanks a hell of a lot, Brent.

It all started several years ago when Brent, then of the Caddis Fly Angling Shop in Eugene, suggested that we get together on a pike trip to northern Idaho where Coeur d'Alene Lake was supposedly overrun with the pugnacious little devils. Reports of 20-pound-plus pike had circulated in recent years and Brent figured we needed to get in on it.

Funny how the "we" part of that didn't include Brent when the actual excursion came about. He weaseled out on a technicality. Unscathed, Timmy—who generally ends up bearing the brunt of a lot of my fly fishing experiments—and I trotted off to northern Idaho. We wanted to fish the pothole-area lakes for bass on the way up there, so we bought Washington licenses. Based on the price, we gathered that the state of Washington is exceedingly proud of its non-resident fishing licenses.

Late that night we arrived at the Super-8 Motel in Coeur d'Alene. The Super-8 was quite proud of its rooms, another fact which we determined based on price. A driving rain gushed forth about midnight and we were glad we had decided on civilized camping instead of our usual recline-the-seats-and-doze-off-to-the-Larry-King-Show-on-A.M.-radio routine.

The next day we spent hours float tubing around various nooks and crannies on massive Coeur d'Alene Lake. The fishing was great; unfortunately, the catching was atrocious. We couldn't buy a pike, or anything else for that matter. Next we tried the Chain Lakes and by some minor intervention by the Saints we managed to avoid being barbecued by a sudden and rather violent lightning storm. Still no pike.

Our second day was spent puttering about in a rented outboard. We cast a fly to every pikey-looking hangout we could find in three different bays and still never saw a fish.

On the fourth little bay we turned into our luck changed. Amongst a dense patch of reeds and stick-ups we spied a big pike. This is exactly what we had been told to look for: "They look like big logs laying back in the weeds waiting for a fish to swim by."

Timmy cut the motor and let the breeze push us into casting range. He then eased the anchor into the water while I uncorked a fly. I stripped a bunch of line off the reel and laboriously cast a huge rabbit-strip Dahlberg Diver toward the fish.

Leery of spooking this beast—which we estimated at 15 pounds—I cast well short. After the ripples cleared, I began stripping the fly back. All the commotion caused by the Diver had no visible effect on the pike. I cast closer. Still nothing. I dropped the huge bug behind the fish and stripped it over his back. No reaction. Tim suggested a wet fly, so I grabbed my second rod, which was rigged with a six-inch-long marabou streamer. I cast several feet off to one side of the fish and stripped the fly past him. "I think that moved it a little!" Tim exclaimed, "Cast closer."

This time I retrieved the fly within three feet of the pike's face and it still refused to eat. Timmy suggested a smaller fly and grabbed his rod, which was armed with a three-inch-long Zonker. He delivered four perfect casts, each one progressively closer. The fourth cast snagged up just behind the fish and wouldn't pull free. Unable to interest the pike anyway, we decided to move in close, thinking we could at least shoot some photos of the fish, that was holding under about four feet of water.

Upon closer inspection, we decided we didn't really need any photos of a 15-pound log laying on the bottom of a lake, so we unhooked Timmy's fly from the log's back and whimpered off to other locales.

At least the day wasn't lacking excitement: A moment after turning the boat directly into the wind and its accompanying two-foot waves, Timmy asked me to fetch him a Gatoraid out of the ice chest. My stumbling toward the front of the boat was punctuated by Tim's steering us directly into the largest wave of the day. The ensuing impact between my right foot and a nice $350 Sage 9-weight rod resonated with a very distinct "CRACK," all too familiar to those of us who have broken rods in foolish ways before.

Utterly pike-less, we puttered back to the dock with our little $50 rental late that afternoon. We were desperate, so I suggested the nearest bar. Tim suggested we could find pike in Montana. I told him I considered them—bars and Montana—to be more-or-less synonymous, so off we went to Montana to search out the mean, snakey, snaggle-toothed beasts. After finding several at a bar in Thompson Falls, we then went in search of pike in Thompson Falls Reservoir.

After two hours of casting practice, I scored. The dumbest pike in Montana pounced on a popping bug and I yarded him in for photos. I handed the whole works—rod, pike and everything—to Tim so I could shoot the pictures. Tim grabbed the little half-pint pike in a strangle-hold that would've made a pro wrestler cry uncle. As the pike's eyes bulged out of their sockets due to Tim's death-grip, I shot a couple quick photos. Before I could snap another shot, however, the pike decided it'd had about enough of this rudeness. One big snakey wiggle and it slipped from Tim's

grip and dropped back into the lake. I couldn't believe it. Three days fishing to catch one pike and all I got was two lousy photos. I suggested that Timmy swim in after that pike and retrieve it; Timmy suggested that I not make any more suggestions.

That fish became known to Timmy and I as the $400 pike. Add up the gas, the food, the motels, the boat, the rod repair and that wonderful Schmidt's beer and that's exactly what that pike cost us. Next time I'll just take the Schmidt's and go home.

Then there was my attempts at taking giant walleye on a fly in the upper Columbia. How's this for fly fishing: You rig up a piece of 800-grain shooting taper attached to monofilament running line. To this you add a three-foot leader and a big lead-head bunny fly. Then you have Oregon's best walleye guide, Mike Jones, run you out to a 50-foot-deep walleye haunt. You start at the top of the hole and toss the fly out. You strip off a bunch of running line until you can feel the lead-head fly ticking on the bottom as you drift downstream at current speed. Then you just drift—it's like back-bouncing plugs in a way except that you are using a fly and fly rod.

I figured we couldn't miss. Mike figured we couldn't miss. We missed. But we had a pretty good time catching alternate species: a yellow perch here and a smallmouth bass there.

Tim Blount and the $400.00 pike taken by the author in western Montana.

On about the second drift through the hole I finally nailed something solid. Whatever the beast from the deep was, it could fight like crazy, swimming in big, pulsing circles. After a time I managed to land the little devil—a freshwater clam of about a pound or so. Snagged you ask? No way. Got him right in the lip. Just to prove it was no fluke, I hooked another a short time later. Luckily I was using barbless flies, so I was able to slip the hook out of the clam's lips and gently ease my vanquished quarry back into the water.

Not long after releasing the second clam, I hooked something much larger. I was certain I'd found my walleye. Turned out to be one hell of a carp. I've heard folks say carp tastes pretty good when it's smoked. Hell, what doesn't taste good smoked? Salt down shoe leather and run it through the smoker and you'd have a reasonable meal. Besides, anyone who says carp tastes good has probably never tried halibut or salmon. It's all relative. I will say this about carp: They fight better than a lot of other freshwater fish, although their efforts seem less spirited than those of the big freshwater clam, whose fight is comparable only to that of the Lucky Lager beer bottle I once caught and landed in Yaquina Bay.

The same year that I perfected my techniques for freshwater clams I began hearing rumors about fly-caught catfish in the Snake River near Nampa. Clayne Baker got to me first with a bunch of fly-rod catfish stories he told me one night before a meeting of the Boise Fly Fishing Club. Then Dave Tucker, who used to own a shop called Streamside Adventures in Boise, finished me off: "You gotta get over here, John. The cats are hitting pretty good down on the river right now."

Timmy and I were leaving for Idaho anyway, so why not try for catfish on the way through. We fished exactly where we were told. We fished the flies we were told to use. Nary a catfish. Smallmouth bass and squawfish aplenty, but no cats.

I'm still not sure when this cruelty will end and I'm not sure what I did to deserve it, but Tucker gets worse every year. This year he called up and said, "John—God, am I glad I caught you. You and Tim better get over here because the catfish are taking dry flies right now!"

Despite my best efforts to steer you clear of such ridiculous pursuits, some among you will no doubt insist upon pursuing pike, carp, catfish and other Northwest myths and legends. All I can say is do your homework first, be wary if your sources include the likes of Dave Tucker and Brent Snow, and if all else fails, have fun.

Tim Blount fly fishes for catfish in the Snake River in western Idaho. Although not visible in this photo, several prominent members of the local fly fishing community are hiding in the bushes across the river rolling around in fits of laughter and occasionally tossing a rock into the river to fool the unwary into thinking catfish are rising for mayflies.